1981

THE SORROW AND THE FURY

THE SORROW
AND
THE FURY

Overcoming Hurt and Loss from Childhood to Old Age

by Lucy Freeman

PRENTICE-HALL, INC.
Englewood Cliffs, New Jersey

The Sorrow and the Fury:
Overcoming Hurt and Loss from
Childhood to Old Age
by Lucy Freeman

Printed in the United States of America

Prentice-Hall International, Inc., London
Prentice-Hall of Australia, Pty. Ltd., Sydney
Prentice-Hall of Canada, Ltd., Toronto
Prentice-Hall of India Private Ltd., New Delhi
Prentice-Hall of Japan, Inc., Tokyo
Prentice-Hall of Southeast Asia Pte. Ltd., Singapore
Whitehall Books Limited, Wellington, New Zealand

10 9 8 7 6 5 4 3 2 1

Library of Congress Cataloging in Publication Data

Freeman, Lucy.
    The sorrow and the fury.

    Bibliography: p.
    1. Bereavement—Psychological aspects. 2. Develop-
mental psychology. I. Title.
BF575.G7F72   155.9'37   78-8533
ISBN 0-13-822908-2

To Lucy Kroll
_____

Friend and literary agent
who suggested this book

Acknowledgments

My thanks to Robert Stewart,
a sensitive and creative editor who helped
me shape this book, and to the following
psychoanalysts for help on the research:
Dr. Lawrence J. Friedman, Dr. Martin Grotjahn,
Dr. Henriette Klein, Dr. George Pollock,
Dr. Gregory Rochlin and Dr. Walter A. Stewart.
Thanks also to Katherine Wolpe, librarian,
and Jeanette Taylor and Ruth M. Reynolds of the
New York Psychoanalytic Institute library.

Foreword

Lucy Freeman, combining her superb skills as a writer, observer of her own feelings and those of others, and as a careful student of literature and psychoanalytic psychology, presents us with a very excellent theoretical and clinically illustrated volume on losses. It can be profitably read by the professional as well as by those introspective beings who wish to know more about themselves.

Joseph Conrad has noted that he who forms a tie is lost. And yet without ties what is man? Ties satisfy, fulfill, and provide self and social security to face life. Yet by virtue of their capacity for acute rupture, dissolution or change, ties render us vulnerable.

Three recently acclaimed films, *Annie Hall, Saturday Night Fever,* and *An Unmarried Woman* have attempted to portray the dilemmas associated with losses and how hope and resolution may be possible. In one, the focus is on developmental loss—the late adolescent who realizes he is ready to dissolve ties with his family, his friends, and his life-style. He painfully looks forward to a new phase of his self-development. In another, two lovers sadly realize they have grown apart with resulting and seemingly irreconcilable differences in goals, values, ideals, and life-style satisfactions. In the last, the abandoned wife is traumatically confronted with the sudden and seemingly unexpected loss of her husband. She goes through an intense mourning process for the seemingly meaningful relationship that is no more. When the chance for a reconciliation presents itself, she realizes she does not want to go back—she has grown and become free. The pull to return to the past, the testing and trying of new means of adapting, the hurts and the newly found joys are worked through and one anticipates newer creative life experiences.

These losses and gains in the cinema, in literature, and poetry are expressions of our time. With family structures different today than before, with the emancipation of those previously enslaved, with individuals living longer and in better physical condition, losses and creative gains will be more in focus.

Lucy Freeman's book explains the loss-gain process. Her clear and succinct case illustrations vividly illuminate the theoretical explanatory and descriptive propositions offered. Her contribution is to be welcomed and its usefulness will be apparent to her readers.

George H. Pollock, M.D., Ph.D.
Director, Chicago Institute for Psychoanalysis
Professor of Psychiatry, Northwestern University

CONTENTS

We are healed
of a suffering
only by experiencing
it to the full.

—*Proust*

Introduction

The vital part loss plays in our lives is only now being explored. Not only the devastating loss we feel when someone we love dies but the loss that underlies loneliness and anxiety. The loss of self-esteem, of dignity. Any loss of everyday life that makes us feel demeaned, humiliated, unloved.

We can save ourselves much heartbreak if we can become aware of our sorrow and fury not only at a current loss but losses that have occurred all through life. For it is our hidden emotional reactions to a loss—whether it be loss of money in the stock market or loss of self-respect when someone we love criticizes us—that keeps us from accepting the loss.

From talking to psychoanalysts and reading books and journals, as well as from my own psychoanalysis, I learned of the

extremely important part losses play in our emotional development. In this book I summarize recent research on how loss
affects our well-being. I also describe how to cope with both the
large and the small losses so they lose their power to hurt.

Any understanding of how loss affects us must start with
Freud's discovery of the emotions involved in loss, which led to
further research. A "mourning process" was discovered, which
had to be fulfilled if a loss were to be accepted. If we do not go
through the mourning process, we will never give up the person
or object lost and are apt to remain depressed. The mourning
process allows us to detach our emotions from what has been lost.
It includes becoming aware of both our grief and our rage, feelings we are apt to hide from ourselves because we believe them
shameful, embarrassing.

The mourning process also carries with it the seeking of
restitution. Unless we find some restitution—another love, a new
interest, be it painting, photography, writing, starting a new
business—we do not fully accept the loss. We must be able to
invest our energy in someone or something new. This means we
are no longer so emotionally tied to the person or object lost.

The anger we repress after a loss holds the key to why we
inflict undue suffering on ourselves. The anger is always followed by guilt. And, for that guilt, we unconsciously punish
ourselves even though the guilt is not based on reality but stems
from our fantasies.

The first great loss of my adult life was the death of my
father. I was thirty-two but the moment I learned of his death, I
became a bereaved child of two. I cried wildly to the heavens,
"Why did this happen to me?" I felt there would now be no one
on earth to love me, to care what happened to me. I thought,
"What's the use of living?"

I was unable to stop longing for him. I mourned way beyond
the natural period of a year. Several years passed and I still felt
lost, thinking irrationally, "If he really loved me, he wouldn't
have died and left me feeling so alone."

On the psychoanalytic couch I slowly became aware my
feelings for my father were not all adoration and love. I recalled
moments I hated him—the few times he slapped me, called me in

childhood such derogatory names as "pest" and "little stinker," or sneered, when I was in my teens, that I had no taste in clothes, dressed like a "tramp."

I had hidden from myself the hatred I had stored against a father who had been somewhat of a tyrant, though a brilliant, charming man. I realized he did not always treat his wife and children as though they were human, entitled to the same feelings he possessed, including the right to independent thinking.

I also realized the powerful pull of the two feelings in ambivalence—love struggling against hate. We are taught as children to repress the hate in order to appear civilized. But hate never stays fully repressed. It keeps trying to emerge in distorted shapes such as physical illness, accident proneness and depression, which is anger turned on the self. Only by becoming aware of the anger—not acting on it but knowing you feel it—can you be free of its destructive effect.

The most difficult part of my analysis was facing the anger and guilt I had buried over the years. I went around with a *mea culpa* attitude, believing I was to blame for the ills of the world. I could lose this masochistic mask only as I became aware of my furious, sometimes murderous feelings at my mother and father. I blamed them, sometimes reasonably, sometimes unreasonably, for what I felt the losses in life that had made me unhappy.

I realized many of my losses were part of growing up. As Dr. Margaret Mahler, world-famous psychoanalyst, told me recently, "Growing up is a continuous process of mourning losses."

Specific losses occur during different periods of our lives. In this book I discuss the losses we face in infancy, childhood, adolescence, married life, middle age and old age. The way we meet each loss is determined by how we have met the losses of the past. If we were not able to accept previous losses, we have to try to face the grief and fury connected to these past losses. For unless you realize losses start in childhood and continue through life and understand, too, you may have been repressing sorrow and resentment at past losses, you may never be able to accept a loss.

There are suggestions throughout the book, especially in the final chapter, on how to face losses. When you were a child, you could only observe how your parents coped with their losses and imitate them. But as an adult you possess the ability to reason. You understand how self-destructive it may be not to face buried feelings so you can more effectively cope with the impact of losses—both the daily losses that cause so much waste of time and energy and the losses of the past that set the pattern for the way you handle a current loss.

Our real losses seem to be increasing—the breakup of homes, high divorce rate, forced retirement. More of us feel the inevitable sense of shock at a loss—"I don't believe this is happening to me!" Then the anguish—"How will I ever endure it?" Then the banishing of painful feelings to the unconscious part of the mind, storehouse of our memories.

But behind the sorrow there is the fury. And until you come to grips with that fury, you cannot free yourself from the guilt that shadows your rage. If you can be honest with yourself, the guilt disappears and you no longer have to punish yourself in devious ways, suffering a loss of self-esteem. You gain the strength to use energy formerly tied up in unfulfilled mourning, to become more creative and happier in your personal life.

I hope the readers of this book will get insights as to how to overcome feelings of sorrow and fury at a loss. And also enjoy the psychological detective work involved in tracking down the clues that led to today's helpful theories on the nature of loss.

1
The
Sense of Loss

Not a day goes by but we feel a loss of some kind. A business associate breaks an appointment. A friend hurls an unkind word. Or we lose a wallet, a credit card, a treasured ring.

With each loss we first feel a slight shock. Then we feel sad, despairing, as though we have parted with something intangible but cherished. Then we feel a tinge of anger either at the one who has inflicted the loss or at ourselves for causing it. Then guilt at the anger.

The very word "loss" plays an important part in our daily lives. We feel a "loss of dignity." A "loss of time." A "loss of faith." A "loss of reputation." A "loss of spirit." Sometimes we are "at a loss for words." Perhaps for a moment we feel we have "lost" our minds. We speak derogatorily of a "loser," tell someone we do not like to "get lost."

There is a close connection between a sense of loss and our emotional well-being. Deep and lasting feelings of loss can lead to a depression. "The greatest poverty is . . . to feel that one's desire is too difficult to tell from despair," as the poet Wallace Stevens put it. Depression may become so desperate it ends in suicide, or suddenly unmask a fury so wild it erupts in murder.

In lesser degree, a pervasive sense of loss can thread through our entire lives. We can live in the mood of loss, prevent ourselves from fulfilling our potentials. Loss can cripple our ability to love fully or to work effectively.

A sense of loss may cause various kinds of aberrant behavior. We may withdraw from the world or, in opposite behavior, throw ourselves into frantic activity. We may lose all appetite or hungrily crave food to fill a void that never vanishes. We may suffer insomnia or sleep the night and day away. Or take to excessive drinking, or drugs or sexual addiction.

Loss may take a toll physically as well as psychically. Our emotions and bodily reactions cannot be separated—this was proved by the historic work of the physiologist Dr. Walter B. Cannon.

Cannon showed that feelings of pain, hunger, fear and rage produce specific changes in our body as it prepares either for "fight or flight." As we feel pain, hunger, fear or rage, sugar pours into our blood for quick energy. Our breath quickens to provide more oxygen. Our muscles tense for immediate use. Our heart races, causing our blood pressure to rise and speed fuel and oxygen throughout the body. Our senses become sharper—the pupils of our eyes dilate so more light can enter, enabling us to observe every dangerous detail in the threatening outer world.

Cannon also introduced the principle of what he called homeostasis. As disturbances upset the body's state of balance, biological processes rush to reestablish the natural states of equilibrium and constancy.

Freud had earlier applied the theory of "constancy," or balance, to the human mind. When we become emotionally upset, mechanisms in our mind automatically set about to restore a psychical sense of constancy.

Freud was the first to observe the connection between a

danger not from the world outside but from the *inside*—the psyche—and its influence not only on the mind but the body. He observed as his patients could release emotional distress through words and feelings, the disappearance of their physical symptoms, ones without organic cause, such as paralysis of a leg or arm, headaches, respiratory infections, stomach pain.

Investigators today are recognizing that a wide range of diseases—perhaps every ailment known to man—may be tied to loss and bereavement. Men and women who lose someone they love may show a change in their growth hormone levels, according to Dr. George L. Engel, professor of psychiatry and medicine at the University of Rochester. Other studies reveal biochemical and neurophysiological changes in the body following the loss of a loved one. Seventy-five out of eighty-seven patients hospitalized for ulcerative colitis reported they suffered a separation from someone they loved just before the illness, according to a study by psychiatrist Dr. Erich Lindemann.

Even cancer is believed related to loss. One hundred adults with blood cancer (either leukemia or lymphoma) were studied by a medical team at the University of Rochester, headed by Dr. William A. Greene. With few exceptions, the cancer appeared when the patient was suffering either a real or a feared loss. In another study of men with leukemia or lymphoma, Dr. Greene discovered the diseases appeared after the loss or separation from a loved one, usually a mother or mother figure.

Physical illness may be one way the body mourns a loss the mind cannot accept. The sentiment "He died of a broken heart" is not as wild as it sounds. Dr. Colin Murray Parkes and his associates studied 4,500 British widowers, fifty-five years and older. The death rate during the first six months after loss of a wife was 40 percent higher than married men the same age. The greatest increase in mortality was due to "heart" disease.

Death rates for men who have lost their wives are consistently higher than those for married people. Higher, too, for men who have lost wives than women who have lost husbands. The death rate for young widowers is double that of young widows. It appears that, for men, the first six months of bereavement are a time of danger. The increase in mortality is not only limited to the widowed but includes close relatives of the lost one.

Most of us, fortunately, do not often experience the severe loss through death of someone loved, which produces uncontrollable, irrational feelings that sweep across us like threatening tidal waves. It is, rather, the day-to-day smaller losses that cause us to feel the stab of indignity—when a promised phone call fails to come through or someone we have always thought loved us suddenly lashes out at us for a trivial mistake.

Everyone suffers losses. As Longfellow said: "If we could read the secret history of our enemies, we should find in each man's life sorrow and suffering enough to disarm all hostility."

When we feel a loss, we suffer mental pain—a drop in self-esteem. Our psychological processes prepare to deal with the pain by "fight or flight." Because we have been taught to act civilized, to repress what may be a murderous feeling, most of the time we restrain the instinct to fight and deny our anger at a loss, turning it on the self. We then feel guilty because of the repressed anger and our self-esteem drops. It is this lowered self-esteem that causes us to feel depressed after a loss.

What is "self-esteem" and why is it connected to a loss? Self-esteem is a feeling vital to our emotional health. When we have little self-esteem we feel unlovable. We think of ourselves as unworthy of love or friendship.

There is a difference between self-esteem and narcissism. Both are part of our instinct of self-preservation, one of our two strongest instincts (the other is our sexual drive). Narcissism is the primitive, unconscious counterpart of the conscious feeling of self-esteem.

We are born narcissistic, a feeling that propels us into saving our emotional lives with fantasy when we feel endangered or confused. As our reason develops we are able to consider the feelings of others as well as our own. Narcissism is now tinged with self-esteem. The adult who always puts himself first, who cannot consider others, is still enmeshed in the narcissistic thrall of childhood. He has never felt emotionally strong enough to develop much self-esteem. The narcissistic person, who is vain, self-centered, is difficult to love. The person with self-esteem, who has confidence, empathy, is lovable.

The higher our feelings of self-esteem, the less likely we are to react to a loss, both the superficial and the severe, with panic and uncontrollable grief. We have learned to depend on our inner resources and we suffer losses less—those inflicted by the outside world, those inflicted by someone we love, and those inflicted by our own fantasies.

Also, the higher our self-esteem, the more likely we are to choose closeness with those who possess self-esteem and are less apt to inflict disappointments and losses on us. It is no accident that many masochistic women who think little of themselves marry men who beat them physically or tear them down verbally, further lowering their self-esteem.

A woman may sadistically destroy a man's self-esteem to the point where he kills her. Many a wife would be alive today had she not sneered at her husband, "You're not a man! You can't even find a decent job." When she accuses him of not being a man, she inflicts on him such a devastating loss of self-esteem he may be driven to murderous fury.

One man who had been married to a woman for ten years suddenly turned on her and knifed her to death. A psychiatrist interviewing the man to diagnose his mental condition, asked, "Why did you kill your wife?"

The man said quietly, "Because she threatened to leave me for another man. She told me I was no good in bed." His wife had deprived him of his self-esteem, caused him to feel an excruciating loss of self.

Why should a top executive, with the power to hire and fire thousands of employees, feel depressed at overhearing a colleague criticize him for poor judgment in a business deal, a criticism not even warranted? The executive overreacts because the criticism triggers memories of a father who accused him of not being "man enough" to succeed in the business world. The executive feels criticism as a loss of essential self-esteem.

We all need the approval of the self. "It may be called the Master Passion, the hunger for self-approval," said Mark Twain.

If we have high self-esteem, when someone is critical or snubs us, we do not take it personally. We realize the one trying to wound us emotionally is projecting his sense of inferiority onto us.

When we suffer a minor loss such as a television set in a robbery or a few days work because we lost our balance and fell on an icy street, self-esteem permits us to think not that such a loss is tragic but merely one of life's vicissitudes we cannot control.

Most important, a feeling of self-esteem allows us to mourn naturally, rather than in a depressed way, a severe loss such as the death of a parent. We will grieve for a year, then accept the loss, rather than suffer years of unfulfilled mourning.

One of the world's leading authorities on the effect of stress on the body, Dr. Hans Selye, professor and director of the Institute of Experimental Medicine at the University of Montreal, advises us not to avoid stress, which he describes as "the very salt and spice of life," but to learn to master and use it.

How can we better master and use the sense of loss we so often feel in everyday life? First let us look at how the experts on human behavior arrived at an understanding of the way losses affect our thoughts and deeds.

2
How
Losses Affect Us

To understand the impact of a loss upon us emotionally, let us consider the discoveries of the man who first studied the effect of a loss on the human mind. He did so in an attempt to ease the suffering caused by a loss, hoping, as the Bible says, "Sorrow and sighing shall flee away."

As a young psychoanalyst Freud could not help but notice how deeply the death of a mother or father affected a son or daughter. The loss often triggered a depression that was lasting or difficult to overcome.

We all feel bereaved at the death of a parent, one of the most, if not the most, tragic losses in life. Our primitive ancestors realized this and did not repress their feelings when a parent died but sobbed and moaned in open grief, sometimes for days. Soci-

25

ety has over the centuries traditionally allowed the mourner one year to "savor his sorrow," as Freud put it. During that year the mourner is not supposed to enjoy himself in any conspicuous way or remarry, if he has lost a mate. It is accepted as natural that he lose interest temporarily in his work, other people and social activities.

Mourning the death of a parent or someone else beloved is a time of external tears and "internal bleeding," to use Freud's phrase. When someone we love dies, at first we feel a sense of unbelievable shock—perhaps even terror at what the future holds without his presence.

We may sob for hours, our body fatigued, drained by tears and emotional pain, agreeing with Don Quixote: " 'Twill grieve me so to heart, that I shall cry my eyes out." We may move in a world that seems unreal, a world in which we feel there is nobody left to love. We may speak of the dead person as though he were alive. We may deny the reality of his death as we walk the streets, see someone who faintly resembles him and think, "Why, there he is. He isn't dead, after all."

Morris Dank, owner of a Brooklyn grocery store, was shot in the head and instantly killed by a thief. The thief became infuriated when Dank blocked his escape from the store, causing him to drop a brown paper bag out of which spilled the $180 he had stolen. Dank's twenty-year-old daughter said, on hearing of her father's murder, "I just don't believe he's gone. I keep expecting him to walk in the door."

Many sons and daughters go through a year or two mourning a dead parent, then resume life as before. But some never recover from the death of a parent. Elvis Presley was one.

Presley announced after his mother's death at the age of forty-two that he would die at the same age. And he unconsciously arranged it so he did. He took pills that destroyed his mind and body. He ate junk foods and grew grossly fat in face and physique. He did not wish to live more years than his mother, so deep his wish to join her, so merged emotionally was he with her. Death was no stranger in his life. A twin brother had died at birth, for which Presley later no doubt felt very guilty. Siblings always hold death wishes for each other—every child wants to be the only child so he can have all his mother's love. When a rival brother or sister actually dies, the surviving child believes his death wishes responsible, such is the world of infantile megalomania.

A brilliant, beautiful actress, the wife of an industrialist, was outwardly a vibrant, appealing woman until the death of her mother. Then she sank into a depression so deep she made several attempts to kill herself. Finally she succeeded, taking an overdose of sleeping pills.

"Why? Why?" her friends asked each other in sadness and wonder. On the surface this woman possessed everything—beauty, intelligence, wealth, a devoted husband, a married son and daughter, three lavish homes. But she had lost her mother and no longer wanted to live.

At the time of the anniversary of a parent's death, sons and daughters may suddenly feel a deep sense of loss, not realizing why. A forty-year-old woman felt mysteriously depressed every year the last week in September. During a session with her psychoanalyst, she mentioned her mother had died when she was ten years old.

"What month of the year?" asked the analyst.

"I don't remember but I'll ask my father," she said.

At the next visit she told the analyst in surprise, "My mother died September twenty-seventh. I had forgotten the month, much less the day."

"It was too painful for you to remember consciously, but your unconscious remembered," said the analyst.

The most famous patient in psychoanalytic history, Anna O. (her real name was Bertha Pappenheim and she was Germany's first noted volunteer social worker), broke down emotionally while her father lay dying and after his death. Dr. Josef Breuer treated her by hypnosis, helping her overcome her desire to kill herself. He encouraged her to express her feelings of grief and anger at the loss of her father. Freud, then a medical student, was told by his friend Breuer how Anna O.'s depression disappeared as she could speak freely of her deeper feelings. Freud later paid tribute to Anna O. for leading him to the technique of free association, which she spoke of as "the talking cure."

In wondering why some sons and daughters, after the death of a parent, were gripped by such a deep sense of loss they also wanted to die, Freud said he suspected more than "pure mourning" was involved if a loss became this overwhelming.

He noted particularly the feelings of guilt as a son or daughter complained, "I could have been a better child." Or, "I should have seen my mother [or father] more when she was ill, alone and facing death." Or they recalled the pain they had caused their parent, which made them feel responsible for the parent's death.

As one woman remarked recently after the death of her sixty-year-old mother, "I know I'm responsible for her dying. I neglected her during her last years, the ones she needed me the most. Why, I wasn't even by her side in the nursing home when she died. I'll never get over my guilt if I live to be a hundred."

The feeling of hate for a parent is especially repressed at those times pity for the parent is paramount, such as when he is ill or dies, Freud pointed out. One of the signs of grief at a parent's death is to reproach the self for the death. Or to punish by putting the self, as retribution, in place of the dead parent, thinking, "It is I who should have died, because I feel so guilty."

Freud made a historic discovery when he observed there was a difference between "natural" mourning after the loss of a loved one and what he called "unnatural melancholic" feelings, part of a depression that will not disappear.

Originally Freud linked depression to a repression of our sexual urges, calling this the sole cause. He noted that many a depressed young girl, who was undeveloped sexually, could not eat, claiming she had no appetite. Freud commented: "Loss of appetite—in sexual terms, loss of libido." (Dr. Karl Abraham, one of Freud's pupils and colleagues, was later to say of depressed persons who overate, "Food has taken the place of love.")

But then, in a letter to his friend Wilhelm Fliess on May 13, 1897, Freud outlined a theory that proved the foundation of all future discussion on loss. He stated that hostile wishes against parents, stemming from childhood, were "an integral part" of the depression that follows a loss.

These hostile wishes come to light consciously in the form of obsessional ideas, he claimed. In paranoia, for instance, the delusions of persecution, the supposed murderous threats by unseen and unknown enemies, arise from the person's wish to kill the parents of infancy whom he feels threatened his life. Because such a wish is dangerous to his emotional survival, it is projected on others.

When a person screams to the world "someone evil" is out to kill him, he is telling us *he* is the "evil" one who wished as a child to kill his mother and father. There is usually what Freud called "a fragment of fact" in the paranoiac's accusation, in that his mother and father brutalized him emotionally.

Our murderous and sexual wishes underlie what Freud described as "psychic reality"—comprised of the countless fantasies in our mind—as opposed to the objective reality of the outer world. It is the opposition of the two worlds in which we live that causes our deepest conflicts.

Freud's last mention of loss and depression in a letter to Fliess appeared on January 16, 1899. Freud wrote that one of the women he was seeing in analysis was continually plunged into despair by "the gloomy conviction" she was useless and good for nothing.

Freud commented of this woman, "I always thought that in early childhood she must have seen her mother in a similar state, in an attack of real melancholia." It is significant that, as early as 1889, he spoke of a mother's depression having an effect on a child. This theory was later elaborated upon by a number of psychoanalysts, including Freud's famous daughter Anna.

The understanding of how a loss affects us came primarily from Freud's penetrating paper "Mourning and Melancholia," written in 1915. He described the important difference between "mourning" and "melancholia," or depression.

He described mourning as the normal emotion of grief to the

loss of a loved person. Or the loss "of some abstraction that had taken the place of the loved one," such as an ideal or the fatherland or liberty.

He noted, however, that some, instead of grieving naturally over a loss, then accepting it, sink into depression, or melancholia. He described melancholia as ". . . a profoundly painful dejection, abrogation [abolishing] of interest in the outside world, loss of the capacity to love, inhibition of all activity, and a lowering of the self-regarding feelings to a degree that finds utterance in self-reproaches and self-revilings, and culminates in a delusional expectation of punishment."

He went on to say the same reactions appear in grief—with one exception. That exception is *the lowering of self-esteem*.

"In grief, the world becomes poor and empty; in melancholia it is the ego itself," as he put it.

Mourning has a psychic purpose, Freud explained—the testing of a reality in which the loved one no longer exists as feelings of love are slowly withdrawn. Bit by bit, "at great expense of time and energy," memories and hopes are relinquished, "usually painfully." When the work of natural mourning is finished, "the ego" once again becomes free and uninhibited and can turn "to another love."

But if "the work of mourning" remains unfinished, if it is not possible for the bereaved person to bestow his love on someone else, grief turns into depression. In other words, upon the death of someone you love, it is normal to mourn for about a year. But if this mourning lasts for years, it is melancholia, or depression.

One man, after his mother died at seventy-three, fell into a depression out of which he could not pull himself. He had never married and realized he had been exceptionally close to his mother, a widow. Her death left him so bereaved he could hardly drag himself to his job as a scenic designer. He finally decided to consult a therapist, who helped him face his deeper feelings about his mother, including those of resentment and anger.

Feelings of depression at a loss other than a loved one's death were mentioned by Freud. He cited the bride left at the altar. He spoke of those who felt depressed but did not know why. He said there were people who knew whom they had lost but not "what in them" they had lost. This suggested, he concluded, that melancholia was, in some way, related to a loss of which the person was not aware, as compared to mourning, where he was conscious of what he had lost.

Freud also studied the feelings of self-accusation present in the depressed person but not in the one who mourned naturally. Freud said: "He [the depressed person] must surely be right in some way and be describing something that corresponds to what he thinks. . . . He really is as lacking in interest, as incapable of love and of any achievement as he says."

The important thing is not whether the depressed person's "distressing self-abasement" is justified in the opinion of others but that in his own lamentations he is correctly describing how he feels. The person has lost his self-respect and there is reason why. He is not alone mourning the lost loved one. He is also mourning *a loss within himself that causes him to feel guilty and ashamed.*

Why is the depressed person guilty because of a loss? Why does his natural mourning turn into lasting depression? Why does a normal process become an abnormal one?

Freud's answer: In addition to loving the lost one, the bereaved person also hates him, a hate that is denied and thus causes a guilt he cannot handle.

The key thought in understanding what happens when we suffer a loss (any loss, not only the death of someone we love) is the effect upon ourselves of "guilt." The degree to which we feel "guilty" determines, in large part, whether we can cope with a loss, large or small, or whether we sink into depression.

Guilt follows the suppression of frequent impulses of hate, which imply desire for revenge. The more violent the impulses for revenge, the more marked the tendency to form fantasies of guilt and the deeper the depression.

One woman, editor at a large publishing company, recalls when she was twenty-one her mother, with whom she had violent quarrels as she grew up, died, and she felt great relief.

The relief was immediately followed by guilt. She felt a daughter was not supposed to feel "relieved" when her mother died. But if there has been deep hatred between parent and child, the child inevitably will feel relieved, then guilty, because of his relief and his repressed rage.

A son or daughter always has feelings of ambivalence toward a parent, Freud asserted. This ambivalence "casts a pathological shade on the grief, forcing it to express itself in the form of self reproaches, to the effect that the mourner himself is to blame for the loss of the loved one, i.e., desired it."

In other words, the greater the hate in the love-hate relationship between child and parent, the greater the child's guilt and the deeper his depression when the parent dies. Where there is less hate, the grief is uncomplicated by guilt.

If a child has grown up with a mother and father who have made him feel unwanted, bad, the child will hate in return, often wishing his parents dead. When they eventually die of natural causes, he will be consumed with guilt because of his earlier wishes (no wish ever disappears from the unconscious). He will be unable to mourn naturally because he is repressing rage and guilt, as well as his true despair.

The guilt feelings arise when our conscience sets itself up against our reason and judges it critically. This is what Shakespeare meant when he wrote, "Thus conscience does make cowards of us all." (Around 326 B.C. Bidpai put it, "Guilty consciences always make people cowards.") Cowards in the sense we cannot face the angry feelings that have caused the guilt. Instead we blame the one we hate.

If you listen to the self-accusations of a depressed person, you realize they do not apply to him but to the one he has loved and lost, who has forsaken him. This explains, Freud said, why the depressed person does not hang his head in shame and show an attitude of humility "as would befit his supposed worthlessness." Instead, he causes others a great deal of trouble, draws attention to himself all the time, perpetually takes offense and behaves as if he were treated with great injustice.

Freud concluded: "All this is possible only because the reactions expressed . . . proceed from an attitude of revolt, a mental constellation which by a certain process has become transformed into melancholic contrition."

Why does the depressed person feel contrite, remorseful? In mourning, the libido, or the energy of love, ordinarily becomes freed after a year and directed to someone else. But in depression, the love remains chained to the lost one with whom there is a deep "identification." Elvis Presley never really "gave up" his dead mother but "identified" with her even unto the date of his death.

The concept of "identification" is a very important one in the theory of loss. Freud defined it as "the earliest expression of an emotional tie with another person."

We learn, as a baby, by identifying with mother and father, consciously and unconsciously copying their behavior, adopting their attitudes, trying to please them by carrying out their very thoughts so they will love us. But if there has been identification with a very depressed or very angry mother or father, this cripples our ability to establish our own identity. Our need to be one with the parent is stronger than our need to separate from him.

This was brilliantly portrayed in the book *Psycho*, by Robert Bloch, which later became a blockbuster of a movie directed by Alfred Hitchcock. The young murderer becomes so identified with his mother he assumes her personality after she is dead, even dressing in her clothes at times, always when he commits murder.

Identification is a way of trying to keep within us emotionally someone we love who, we believe, is lost to us. Freud gave the example of a little boy, bereft over the death of his kitten, who announced *he* was the kitten and crawled about on all fours. Many a child, fearing he has lost his mother's love as he sees brothers and sisters take his place in her arms, may identify with his mother as a way of keeping her all to himself in his imagination.

A child "identifies" through a mental mechanism called "introjection." We may think of it as a psychic swallowing— emotional cannibalism.

A small boy whose mother leaves him alone much of the time, who is terrified by the frequent separations, psychically "incorporates" her so he may at least possess her in fantasy.

What psychoanalysts call "oral incorporation" represents one of the most primitive forms of an ambivalent relationship. It is felt as a method both of destroying and of preserving the loved one. The child yearns for the absent mother who will care for him but at the same time wishes her dead for deserting him when he needs her. He loves/hates both his real mother and the image of her now locked within.

An example of introjection is provided by the analysis of depression, Freud said. Persons depressed at a loss "show us the ego divided, fallen into two pieces, one of which rages against the second." The second piece "has been altered by introjection and contains the lost object." The rage is based on reproaches of the loved/hated lost one and represents "the ego's revenge upon it."

When threatened by the loss of someone he loves, the person who can love only in a childish, narcissistic way may regress to primitive stages of his psychosexual development. We all go through four stages: first the oral, then the anal, then the phallic, and finally the genital.

"Regression" means a return to an earlier level of emotional satisfaction. It is as though we say to ourselves when we feel in psychic pain, "This conflict facing me is too tough. I will retreat to an earlier, less difficult time of life."

One woman whose mother died found she could not stop eating. She gained forty pounds in half a year. She told a friend, "All the will power in the world doesn't help me to control my voracious appetite. I just keep stuffing food into myself to fill the emptiness I feel at my mother's death."

Her friend, who also had lost a mother, replied, "You eat—I drink. My consumption of scotch is keeping me broke. But I need a few drinks every night so I can fall asleep. Otherwise I just lie there feeling sorry for myself."

These women are trying to cope with their grief and resentment at the loss of a parent in a destructive way because they are denying deeper feelings. They are repressing both their sorrow and their fury.

When we feel anger after a loss but repress the anger, we may wish to destroy the person in fantasy with our mouths (the sadistic aspect of the oral stage—biting) and with fury and spite (from the anal stage). Such sadism, felt after a loss, Freud said, solves what he called "the enigma of suicide."

We cannot find the emotional energy needed to kill ourselves unless we are also in fantasy killing someone we hate and with whom we identify, Freud held. Our ego can destroy itself only if, owing to the strength of the loved one as retained within as image, our ego treats itself as though it *were* the loved one. The ego then directs against itself all the rage it feels for the loved one who has abandoned it.

In Freud's words, "the shadow of the object—the loved-hated one—falls upon the ego." The shaded part of the ego is then criticized as though it were the hated part of the loved one. Freud noted that in the two opposite situations of falling passionately in love and feeling suicidal, the ego is overwhelmed by the loved one, though in totally different ways. (Freud once stated, "One is very crazy when one is in love.")

Thus "each man kills the thing he loves" but only if he also hates. Oscar Wilde must have hated deeply the mother of his infancy, the mother to whom he was so attached he never dared love another woman. The suicide kills (forever loses) that part of himself identified with the loved/hated one as he turns on himself his overwhelming guilt because of his murderous wishes.

One woman left as suicide note: "I hate my mother, a tyrannical, domineering woman who does not allow me to draw my own breath. I wish she were dead, which means I am a wicked child and deserve as punishment what I wish as her fate."

She felt she and her mother were in part merged. Dr. Walter A. Stewart, psychoanalyst, recently told me:

"It is when you hate the other person, as well as love him, and feel merged with him, that you can kill yourself—the self being indistinguishable from the other person. The wish to murder is fully gratified when someone commits suicide. It is as if he killed the other person as he kills himself. It doesn't really matter which one he kills. In his unconscious it is death to both."

The presence of hate followed by guilt, in the conflict between love and hate, causes depression. The main purpose of depression, Stewart notes, is to handle aggression in a regressive way by turning the aggression back on the self because there *is* love. Otherwise, the hate would triumph and murder would result. The one who murders has experienced so little love and so much violence and hate in childhood that eventually his repressed murderous feelings explode. In the case of suicide, the final loss—loss of one's life—the hate overpowers the love.

A boy in his senior year at a prep school was jilted by a girl with whom he had fallen desperately in love. He hanged himself from a bar in his closet. He left a note to the girl: "I cannot live without you. Since you choose to reject me, I have no choice but to die."

A friend of the family noted this was a youth abnormally attached to a mother who made it difficult for him to break away from her, phoning the private school every night to make sure he was "all right." The boy, in fantasy, wrote the suicide note to his mother, telling her he could not live without her by his side. Though he had left her, he felt it as her rejection, believing in some way she should have stopped him. Most boys, if jilted by a girl, would easily find another love.

Any act as destructive as suicide has its roots in infancy. It comes out of the relationship between mother and child in which the child feels the victim of emotional cruelty. As Elizabeth Barrett Browning wrote: "The child's sob in the silence curses deeper than the strong man in his wrath."

The child who feels unloved—as a child tied too tightly to his mother essentially feels, for she constricts his independence—will hate his mother even as he yearns for her, turning the hate inward. The hatred simmers over the years as he unconsciously chooses to love someone similar to his mother. When they reject him, he hates them, too, and if the guilt becomes intolerable he may kill himself.

Suicides often have the conscious fantasy of revenge on the lost loved one just before they kill themselves. They think, "He will feel guilty because I am dead," expressing the hope the life of the one who has hurt and deserted them will be destroyed by guilt and remorse. Notes left by suicides speak of a desire for vengeance, the wish their death will "haunt" the villain who has jilted them.

Mourning the loss of a loved one is a normal emotional process, according to Freud. He said it had "a quite specific psychical task to perform: its function is to detach the survivor's memories and hopes from the dead. When this has been achieved, the pain grows less and with it the remorse and self-reproach."

But many of those memories have to do with anger. And "hostility to the dead is not easily tolerated by the mourning ego," in the words of Dr. George H. Pollock, director of the Institute for Psychoanalysis in Chicago and past president of the American Psychoanalytic Association.

We recoil from anything that is painful and mourning is painful in many ways. When we think of another's death, it reminds us that someday we too will die. Lately there has appeared popular interest in mourning, death and dying. Perhaps after the sexual revolution, in which our erotic repressions were given release, the only thing left to face is the repression of our fear of death and dying.

Let us apply Freud's significant discovery of the difference between "natural mourning" and "depression" following loss of a parent through death to other losses in life.

Let us find out what occurs during the process of natural mourning to enable us to separate ourselves emotionally from who or what has been loved and lost.

For if we are unable to complete the mourning process, the loss may haunt us forever.

3
The Mourning Process

We all know men and women who have spent their lives in obvious mourning over a dead parent or a dead lover. One woman of fifty-nine, a noted writer, has never married, she says, because the only man she ever loved was killed on a Korean battlefield.

Such a woman has not completed the work of mourning that would allow her to separate emotionally from her lost love.

What does this work of mourning entail? Freud first spoke of it. Other psychoanalysts studied in depth what is now called the mourning process as they amplified Freud's theories.

They discovered the mourning process does not suddenly spring into being when someone we love dies. Mourning is an adaptive process that starts in childhood and develops over the years.

The first to connect the depression of an adult following a loss to a "primal depression of infancy" was Dr. Karl Abraham, a colleague of Freud. Abraham asserted that any adult who becomes depressed at a loss rather than naturally mourning it must have gone through a primal depression that preceded and set the pattern for the adult depression. He stated:

"In the last resort . . . [the adult depression] is derived from disagreeable experiences in the childhood of the patient."

Like Freud, he stressed in a loss the importance of ambivalence and the subsequent depression. Feelings of love and hate in the depressed person seemed almost equal as they pulled against each other, and the result was a paralysis of feeling.

As one woman expressed it, after the death of a husband whom she openly despised during the last years of their marriage: "I tried to hold back my rage at him when he became ill. I felt practically catatonic. There were moments I thought I could not move my limbs to go out shopping, or even to give him his medicine."

The hatred in adult depression, originally felt during the primal depression, is directed chiefly against the mother, the important person in one's life at the time of the primal depression, Abraham stated.

When we are a child we feel destructive wishes against our mother when she frustrates us, which she is bound to do, being human and thus imperfect at times. Even as we wish to destroy her, we feel we must save her from destruction, for if she vanishes, who is left to feed and care for us? So we are apt to turn our rage inward and feel depressed because of our guilt.

We show rage at every psychic stage as our losses occur. Our earliest anger is called "oral hostility," since it occurs at the time of life when our mouth is the most important organ. With it we explore the world, using it for the pleasure it gives in sucking and biting, and to show pain when we are hungry by screaming through it. When we are pleased, we smile with our mouth.

The depressed person, acutely feeling a loss, may regress to this oral stage, taking to drink, the swallowing of pills or extreme attitudes about food, either refusing to eat or stuffing himself out of a fear of starving. When we drink or eat excessively, in addition to expressing early repressed anger, we are also satisfying ourselves sexually in an infantile, oral way, Abraham observed. This explains why the overeater, the undereater (who denies his oral hunger and rage), the alcoholic, the drug addict and the pill taker, usually do not possess a strong desire for sex. Their addiction fulfills the erotic needs of the infant stage to which they have regressed in fantasy.

One wife noticed that her husband, after the death of his older brother, to whom he had always been close, started to overeat. He put on fifty pounds in a year. At the same time, he started to withdraw from her sexually. She felt very rejected and went to a psychoanalyst for a consultation. The analyst told her, "Often, after the death of a loved one, the sexual pleasures of an adult are given up temporarily as the person regresses to the precursors of those pleasures in infancy—to drinking or eating in an excessive manner."

"Will my husband get over his insatiable craving for food and want sex again?" she asked worriedly.

"If he can face both his grief and anger at the death of his brother," said the analyst.

The wife persuaded her husband to see a therapist. He gradually ceased overeating, lost weight and again felt sexually attracted to his wife. He had become aware of feelings underlying his addiction.

Abraham explained the depressed person's capacity for love and sex is reduced to a minimum because of his basic hostile attitude. He uses energy normally placed in service of erotic urges to repress his hatred. As Abraham said, "His libido has disappeared from the world, as it were."

He described one patient who, shortly after becoming engaged, was overcome by an inability to feel love and became severely depressed. Abraham noted this happened to several men and women. In each instance he found unconscious hatred from childhood toward a parent was paralyzing the capacity to love and carry through on sexual desire.

The very depressed person, suffering a loss he is unable to mourn, feels hated and believes himself inferior and defective, according to Abraham. He seeths inwardly with a violent desire for revenge which he does not dare put into action and barely allows himself to feel. He ascribes his feelings, in Abraham's words, to "the torturing consciousness" of his own defects instead of to his "imperfectly repressed sadism." He tends to draw the same conclusion as Shakespeare's Richard III, who lists all his failings with pitiless self-cruelty and then states:

> *And therefore, since I cannot prove a lover . . .*
> *I am determined to prove a villain.*

Abraham was the first to relate drug addiction to loss and depression. The drug addict clings to his drugs "with the same despair shown by the depressed person clinging to his image of the lost loved one," Abraham stated.

An eighteen-year-old drug addict was recently asked by a social worker, "Why must you take drugs?"

"I feel lost," she said. "Empty. Lonely."

"What would happen if you gave up the drugs?" asked the social worker.

"I couldn't bear life," she said. "I need the drugs to get me through the day and the night."

"Why do you feel so desperate?"

"I always have," she said. "Even as a little girl I felt there was no one in the world who cared for me after my father left us."

"How old were you then?"

"About six. But I remember he was much kinder to me than my mother ever was. He really loved me. And after he was gone, I had nothing. Now I have my drugs. At least some of the time I feel good."

She was, as Abraham put it, "clinging" to drugs "with the same despair" she felt when her father left home, "clinging" to the image of the only person in her life she believed loved her.

Abraham differed from Freud only in thinking he did not stress the underlying sadistic feelings in depression. This sadism rose from the oral stage and the primal depression caused when a child, feeling unloved by his mother, became furious. His feelings of guilt are later shown in a display not of sadism but masochism, the self-pity that is part of every depression.

A special kind of depression in infancy after a loss was named "the anaclitic depression" by Dr. René Spitz. It followed an infant's separation from his mother at a time he could not cope emotionally with the separation. This depression was seen in babies deserted by their mothers, who spent the first months of their lives in hospitals or other institutions.

If there is a complete absence of mothering, the loss is usually so devastating it equals "emotional starvation," in Spitz's words. It "leads to a progressive deterioration engulfing the child's whole person." The child becomes like the infant monkey who, deprived of his mother, sits huddled in a corner of the cage refusing to move, a starved, pitiful look on its pinched face.

Spitz made the distinction that we feel one kind of loss as a child when a mother dies or abandons us and another kind of loss when she sinks into a depression. The depressed mother gives her child the feeling of an "emotional loss," Spitz said. He explained:

"The mother, in changing her emotional attitude . . . radically changes the signals which identified her as good object for the child. Physically, she remains the same mother she was. Emotionally, the good mother . . . the person whom the child loves, is lost."

Every infant sees his mother in two images—the "good" and the "bad." The two images remain separate until, fusing good and bad, he can consider her a total human being. The depressed mother, ineffectually coping with her own losses, blocks this normal development, Spitz asserted. He maintained every child will "follow the mother into the depressive attitude."

Three stages of the mourning process evolved from observations of small children by Dr. John Bowlby of the Tavistock Child

Development Research Unit in London, famed for its psychological studies of children.

He noted the emotional reactions of children between six months and six years, separated from mothers who could not care for them continuously because of economic or emotional reasons. The children were placed for limited stays in residential nurseries or hospital wards, cared for by strangers for short periods of time, then returned to their mothers, some temporarily, others permanently.

In disclosing his findings Bowlby explained the importance of the loss of a mother during childhood. In the earliest months of life, he said, we learn to discriminate among the figures that pass before our crib, developing a strong liking for one figure, our mother. Throughout the last half of our first year, and during the whole of our second and third years, we become closely attached to her. We are what Bowlby describes as "content in her company and distressed in her absence." We protest all momentary separations. From our first birthday on, a father or brother or sister may also be important, but never as important as the mother. Most of us are fortunate enough to suffer little disruption of this first, very deep attachment.

Bowlby discovered that the child who was fifteen to thirty months when the separation from his mother occurred, who had a "reasonably secure relationship" with her and had not previously been parted from her showed "a predictable sequence of behavior." The child went through phases of "protest, despair and detachment"—what appeared a normal mourning process. In Bowlby's words:

At first with tears and anger he demands his mother back and seems hopeful he will succeed in getting her. This phase of Protest may last several days. Later he becomes quieter, but to the discerning eye it is clear that as much as ever he remains preoccupied with his absent mother and still yearns for her return; but his hopes have faded and he is in the phase of Despair. Often these two phases alternate: hope turns to despair and despair to renewed hope. Eventually, however, a greater change occurs. He seems to forget his mother so that when she comes for him he remains curiously uninterested in her, and may seem even not to recognize her. This is the phase of Detachment.

In each of the three phases the child is prone to tantrums and episodes of destructive behavior, often of a "disquieting violent kind," Bowlby notes. On the child's return home, his behavior depends on the phase reached during his period of separation. Usually, he is unresponsive and undemanding for a while. To what degree, and for how long, depends on the length of the separation and the frequency of the visits made by his mother. When he has not been visited for a few weeks or months, and has reached the early stages of detachment, he will be unresponsive for periods from an hour to a day or longer. But when the detachment does break, his emotions become intense.

"There is a storm of feeling, intense clinging and, whenever his mother leaves him, even for a minute, acute anxiety and rage," reports Bowlby. For weeks, even months, the child may demand his mother's presence at all times and reproach her angrily when she leaves him, fearing to lose her again.

When the infant has been separated from his mother for more than six months, or when separations have been so repeated he has reached the advanced stage of detachment without going through the other two stages, he may never recover affection for his mother, Bowlby says.

He concludes: "There is, indeed, good reason to believe that the sequence of responses—Protest, Despair and Detachment—is a sequence that, in one variant or another, is characteristic of all forms of mourning."

Bowlby calls this process "healthy mourning" when it occurs in an adult. Adults, too, he said, must go through the three phases of mourning, phases that overlap and intertwine. In both adults and children, the mood varies from an immediate expectancy, at first expressed in an angry demand for the person's return, to a despair shown in "subdued pining," or not expressed at all. Though alternating hope and despair may continue, some measure of emotional detachment from the one lost eventually develops. Then follows acceptance of the permanent absence of the lost loved one.

This normal process, however, Bowlby warns, cannot be

completed by a child because the loss occurs when he is too vulnerable, too desperately in need of a loving attachment, to handle the devastating feelings aroused. The child goes through unhealthy, or pathological, mourning. If the loss of a mother occurs at too early an age, without a loving substitute, the child is permanently damaged emotionally, suffering a "grief . . . [that] is a peculiar amalgam of anxiety, anger and despair following the experience of what is feared to be irretrievable loss," in Bowlby's words.

One mother, when her son was two years old, had to leave him with a neighbor for three months when she went to a distant city to care for her ailing mother, in the last stages of cancer. On her return, she became aware the little boy treated her as a stranger and it took months before he would accept her with trust or affection.

When her son was in high school, he started having difficulties with his studies. She sent him to a therapist who discovered the boy was suffering from unexpressed grief and rage over the earlier separation from his mother. The therapist helped him become aware of his sorrow and resentment and also to accept the fact his mother had no choice but to leave him at the time her mother was critically ill.

In Anna Freud's discussion of Bowlby's work on separation, grief and mourning, she questions the use of the term "mourning" applied to infants. She maintains mourning—the painful, gradual process of detachment of love from an internal image—cannot be expected to occur before "object constancy" is experienced, usually about six months of age. "Object constancy" refers to the infant's ability to conjure up the image of a temporarily absent person. The person has become more than just a caretaker and because the infant misses him, he re-creates the person in his imagination.

Anna Freud grants the nearer to the object constancy state, the longer the duration of the infant's brief reactions to loss and the closer this corresponds to the adult's internal process of mourning. But, she claims, the immature personality structure of the infant or older child is not capable of producing the same state of depression as in the adult.

The ego has to be strong enough for mourning to take place,

in the opinion of Dr. Helene Deutsch. Otherwise there is anxiety and regression to earlier states, or a mobilization of defenses that try to protect the ego from distintegration. She calls the "omission" of emotion, such as a child's indifference following the death of a parent, the most extreme expression of the defensive operation of the psyche.

One boy of six, when his father was killed in an automobile accident, showed no signs of grief. He did not shed a tear at the funeral ceremonies. His mother kept asking, "Don't you feel like crying?"

"No," he said gravely.

"What are you feeling?" she asked.

"Nothing," he said.

According to Deutsch, such indifference occurs because a child's ego is not sufficiently developed to bear the strain of the work of mourning. Therefore the ego resorts to "some mechanism of narcissistic self protection to circumvent the process." She suggests this indifferent attitude was also the way the little boy reacted when he first separated from his mother.

A child's ego is not as strong as an adult's. The child cannot use reason. He will react violently to a loss. Consider how a child screams when you take a toy away, much less his mother. As a child grows, he becomes afraid of his violence, fearing punishment by the adults who control him, who usually scold him for expressing anger at a loss. Thus he is apt to repress both his fury and despair, retreating prematurely into detachment. This means he will mourn his whole life for a loss he is never able to accept.

This is particularly true of orphans and children who have grown up in institutions or foster homes, never allowed to mourn the loss of their real parents. They will always suffer from unfulfilled mourning.

It is not to condone, but to understand, something of the murderer in David Berkowitz, who calls himself "Son of Sam," to point out he suffered tragic losses as an infant. He was illegitimate, given away at birth by his mother and father, who later married. After he was arrested, while awaiting trial, his real mother, Betty Falco, wanted to see him but he refused at first to allow her near. It was reported he felt very hurt several years before when he sought her out and found she had a legitimate daughter. His adoptive parents also had a natural daughter, with whom he grew up. His foster mother, to whom he was attached in a strong love-hate relationship (he is reported to have been violent as a boy, smashing furniture and pulling down curtains), died when he was fourteen after a long bout with cancer. According to family friends, this was an emotional shock to the boy. His murderous rages at couples necking in parked cars may have been sparked by his hatred and jealousy of young girls (the two sisters who were legitimate), especially when they were being embraced and loved. This is not to imply early losses of a parent lead to murder but to point out that many emotionally deprived children never overcome the severe losses that overwhelm them and end up destroying themselves or others later in life.

Anger is the first and the immediate, "perhaps invariable," response to the loss of a loved one, Bowlby asserts. The evidence makes it clear, he adds, that anger at the one who is lost is an integral part of the mourning process.

This anger appears to serve the purpose of adding drive to strenuous efforts both to recover the lost loved one and to dissuade him from deserting again, he says. These efforts he calls "the hallmarks of the first phase of mourning."

It is crucial to accept that anger is present in the mourning process, Bowlby holds. Citing the tendency of some psychoanalysts to regard such anger as pathological, he says:

I believe this to be profoundly mistaken. So far from being pathological, the evidence suggests that the overt expression of this powerful urge [anger], unrealistic and hopeless though it may be, is a necessary condition for mourning to run a healthy course. Only after every effort has been made to recover the lost object, it seems, is the individual in a mood to admit defeat and to orient himself afresh to a world from which the loved object is accepted as irretrievably missing. Protest, including an angry demand for the object's return and reproach against it for deserting, is as much a part of the adult's *response to loss, especially a sudden loss, as of the young child's.*

It is not difficult to understand why the reactions of anxiety and protest, despair and disorganization, detachment and reorganization, are the rule for both animals and humans, Bowlby says. In the wild, to lose contact with the family is extremely dangerous, especially for the young, who cannot protect themselves against attack by enemies. It is in the interest of the survival of the individual, both for his own safety and so he will live to reproduce the species, that there exist strong bonds tying together the members of a family. This requires that at every separation, however brief, a person or animal respond by "an immediate automatic and strong effort" both to recover the lost one, especially if it is the mother, the member to whom attachment is closest, and to discourage the mother from ever leaving again.

For this reason, Bowlby suggests, "the inherited determinants of behavior (often termed instinctual) have evolved in such a way that the standard response to a loss of a loved one are always urges first to recover it and then to scold it."

If the futile effort to recover the lost object and angry reproaches against it for deserting are not signs of pathology, in what ways does pathological mourning differ from healthy mourning? Bowlby asks.

He answers: Two of the characteristics of pathological mourning are the inability to express openly the wish to recover the lost object and to express anger at its loss.

Instead of open expression of anger, which leads to a healthy outcome, the urges to recover and reproach, with their mixed feelings of love and hate, become repressed. Unable to find direct expression, they may influence our behavior in strange and distorted ways.

Both in the childhood mourning of a loss and in the pathological mourning of a loss in later years, "the development of the defense process is accelerated," according to Bowlby. He adds that as a result of this early and speeded-up building of defenses, "the urges to recover and to reproach the lost object have no chance to be extinguished and instead persist [in repressed form] with consequences that are serious."

If the mourning process is not completed, two psychic defenses come into play—*fixation* and *repression*. A child will remain "fixated" on a lost mother as both his urges to recover and reproach her and his mixed emotions of love and hate connected with these urges undergo repression. The popular word "hang-up" describes what psychoanalysts call "fixated."

Another defensive process that follows a loss is called splitting of the ego. One part of the personality denies the loved one is lost, maintaining either there is still communication or the lost one will soon be recovered. Simultaneously, another part of the personality admits to the world the person is irretrievably lost. These two parts seem incompatible but they can coexist and, if intense, may lead to severe emotional disturbance.

A forty-five-year-old woman who had never married but lived with her mother, whom she supported, went into shock when her mother died. She refused to believe her mother dead and spoke of her as though she still lived in the house. She set a place for her mother at the dining table and talked to her as though her mother were sitting at it.

This woman's married sister tried to convince her their mother was dead. The woman treated her sister as though *she* were hallucinating, saying, "I know you mean well, dear, but I can see Mother as clearly as I can see you. And hear her when she talks to me."

She was sent to a private psychiatric hospital where she was helped to face her acute grief and anger at the mother who had deserted her, the mother to whom she had been abnormally close. She was able, gradually, to accept the reality of her mother's death.

Bowlby thus described the specific psychological process involved in mourning through which, he said, we must go if we are to accept a loss. A sequence of psychic processes is set in motion by the loss of a loved one. The sequence starts with a craving for the person lost. Then grief, with appeals for help in recovering the lost one. Then anger at the desertion. After the various phases take place, the loss can be accepted.

Is Bowlby's description of the young child's reaction to loss the same as the mature, fully developed mourning process in adults?

This question is asked by Dr. George Pollock, whose own

research over the past two decades has concentrated on exploring many facets of the fundamental mourning process. He has written extensively about mourning and adaptation and the relation of mourning to creativity.

The mourning process is a normal, universal, adaptive process found in all people and throughout history, he stated in the article "Process and Affect: Mourning and Grief." He presented an abridged version at the Thirtieth Congress of the International Psycho-Analytical Association in Jerusalem, August 23, 1977. The article will be published in a forthcoming issue of *The International Journal of Psychoanalysis*.

The mourning process has its own line of development, beginning in early life and reaching maturity after adolescence, when the psychic apparatus is fully developed, Pollock says. The mourning process has evolved through the evolution of man as an adaptive means of dealing with loss, disappointment and change.

In the infant, the earlier and more primitive stages of the mourning process are evident, Pollock says. As the psychic apparatus develops, later stages of the process come into being and are used whenever the mourning process is set in motion.

The mourning process, Pollock states, is initiated by the early experiences of separating from the mother. If these experiences include anxiety, fear, sadness and anger, these feelings are apt to be part of all future reactions to loss.

Some psychoanalysts believe mourning starts in adolescence, when "trial mourning" becomes a precursor of mature mourning. But, according to Pollock, adolescents appear to show defenses against expressing the overwhelming trauma of the loss, rather than mourning the loss. He says: "Perhaps it is only with the completion of adolescence that one is capable of completing the entire mourning process as we characteristically see it in the adult. In younger individuals they may only have attained and are capable of experiencing that part of the mourning process that the development of their psychic apparatus allows."

There is vast difference between the adult who was depressed as a child and is unable to mourn his losses and the adult whose childhood was fairly free of depression, Pol-

*lock says. The adult who felt depressed as a child will find
his depression after a loss, lasting and severe. The adult
with the happier childhood will be able to face his grief and
anger, accept his loss.*

   *"An ego that has developed to the point where reality
is correctly perceived, and objects distinctly and uniquely
differentiated, will mourn differently from an ego that is
poorly integrated and immature," according to Pollock.*

   *Put another way: if a child's relationship to his mother
has been a warm, loving one and he has not been threatened
by the natural losses he encounters, he is likely as an adult
to accept losses without anxiety.*

Pollock points out that mourning is not the same as bereavement,
which he calls "a specific subclass of the mourning process occurring after a meaningful person has died."

   He believes "all change involving 'the loss' of something
and 'the gain' of the new, entails a mourning process that may be
brief, non-conscious and in telescopic fashion including affects
associated with the process." The word "affect" means an emotion and the thoughts, both conscious and unconscious, associated with the emotion.

   One woman, who had lived in New York City for twenty
years, moved to a suburb with her husband and children. As she
packed, she found tears in her eyes. She loved the city and
regretted leaving it, at the same time looking forward to the more
relaxing life of the country.

   She was losing a way of life she had enjoyed and was
mourning the loss, even as she felt she was gaining a new kind of
life she would equally enjoy.

   Pollock believes four outcomes of a mourning process are
possible: (1) a normal resolution with a creative outcome, as the
work of mourning allows for the acceptance of reality; (2) an
arrest of the mourning process during its developmental period;
(3) a fixation at an early point in the process due to excessive
trauma or other factors and to which regression later in life occurs; and (4) a pathological or deviated mourning process that is
closely, though not exclusively, related to melancholia, the de-

pressive disorders and "their potentially lethal outcomes."

He points out the mourning process is also linked with many other developments in the psychic apparatus, though for the purpose of research, the mourning process has been studied as though existing by itself. Its "linkages" extend to all aspects of psychic functioning, "some more and some less significant than others."

He notes that the various stages of the mourning process are accompanied by biochemical and physiological alterations in the body that can be measured. He mentions that group mourning processes and/or defenses against them are found in individuals, groups, associations and even nations. There are those who say the United States is going through a mourning process for the losses it caused and suffered in the Vietnam War.

The mourning process is clearly seen during psychoanalysis. The work of analysis is similar to, at times identical to, mourning work, as the process of detachment and separation occurs, Pollock points out. This is experienced during the analysis not only at times of separation or termination but in the unfulfilled mourning for childhood losses, a mourning that must be fulfilled with the help of the analyst before the analysis can proceed.

While there are similarities in the overall mourning that is the universal adaptation to a loss, there are also some significant differences, Pollock points out. The type of loss must be considered. A permanent loss through death may have quite a different impact from a temporary separation. An unexpected death may be more of a shock than the long-awaited death of a chronically ill parent or mate. The impact on a child of the death of a parent differs from the impact on an adult. The death of the mother during the Oedipal stage of a girl may have a different effect from that on a boy, in that the girl's guilt will be more intense because of her natural death wishes for her rival mother. The death of a brother or sister in childhood will differ in impact from the death of a mate. The loss of a child can never be fully integrated and totally accepted by the mother or father.

Overcoming the defenses against the mourning process must be distinguished from the process itself. Denial of the loss through obsessive replacement of the lost one, for instance, is different from accepting the loss and then freely giving love to another person.

One wife, after her husband of fifteen years told her he had fallen in love with another woman and wanted a divorce, felt agonized but could not face her grief and anger. She merely said, "Do what you want. I won't ask you to stay with me if you're in love with someone else."

She frantically set out to find another man with whom to have an affair as solace. The man she chose satisfied her sexually and she no longer felt so bereft. After a short while she discovered she did not like this man but had a difficult time getting him out of her life. She had not selected a successor to her husband on the basis of love but out of a desperate need to defend herself against feelings of devastation and rage at her husband's infidelity and abandonment.

The men and women who become promiscuous after the loss of a loved one show this same need to run away from dangerous feelings and find comfort in the arms of one person after another. Such obsessive substitution for the lost one is a way of avoiding the mourning process so a more mature choice of mate may be made. Those who try to escape painful feelings after a loss know only what the poet Thomas Gray spoke of as "Grim-visag'd comfortless Despair."

Psychoanalysts agree that how we mourn current losses reflects the way we have mourned, or failed to mourn, our earlier losses. Each current loss awakens remembrance of losses past.

What are these earlier losses? Losses we all have to face: normal, natural losses that occur in the life of every child as he grows up, whether he lives in an African jungle or a Manhattan penthouse.

4
Our
First Losses

Mankind's first recorded loss was of Paradise. The loss of a personal paradise *is* our first loss as a baby—the paradise of living with our every need taken care of.

Perhaps the paradise started even before birth, when we were snug and warm inside our mother's body, until forced out into a cold world where we emitted our first cries at the discomfort of it, the need to breathe and struggle for ourselves. Possibly the cruelest cut of all is that of the umbilical cord.

In 1877 in his essay "A Biographical Sketch of an Infant," Charles Darwin described the observations he made thirty-seven years earlier about one of his children. He said that as early as eleven weeks of age the baby's cries due to hunger, pain or suffering could be differentiated. He wrote, "An infant understands to a certain extent, and I believe at a very early period, the meaning or feelings of those who tend him, by the expression of their features.''

Fear, believed by Darwin to be one of the first feelings experienced by infants, was seen when his baby was only a few weeks old and was followed by crying. Darwin noted ''Pleasurable Sensations'' were associated with sucking and looking at the mother and accompanied by smiling at forty-five days of age. Affectionate behavior appeared before the infant was two months of age. At about six months, there were signs of depression.

Every step of growth carries with it some sense of loss. As Emerson put it, ''For every thing you gain, you lose something.''

The first sense of loss comes as we detach ourselves more and more from our mother. We go through a loss when we are weaned. When we are toilet-trained. When we learn to walk. When we attend nursery school or first grade. The first losses of life may be long out of consciousness but they live on within us. They affect our behavior if we have not been able to mourn them naturally.

Certain normal losses should occur at specific times in growth. If a mother does not wean a child until he is two years old, she is making it very difficult for him to separate from her emotionally. If she weans him at three months, she is also causing him a deep sense of loss.

In a general sense, life's first large loss is the loss of trust in the mother. Since our world as a child revolves around our mother's every move, she becomes to us either a person who protects us, whom we can trust, or someone who endangers us, someone we cannot trust.

What is *trust*? According to Webster's New World Dictionary: ''firm belief or confidence in the honesty, integrity, reliability, justice, etc., of another person or thing; faith; reliance.'' And: ''confident expectation, anticipation, or hope: as, have *trust* in the future.''

Most of us spend our lives searching for someone we can love and trust. Or wishing we could trust ourselves more in the making of decisions along the way of the uncertain years.

Trust has to be built. It develops from childhood on. There is vast difference between the trust of a child, naïve and innocent, who *must* trust his mother and father because they are all he knows of humans, and the trust of an adult, supposedly rational and thoughtful, able to choose those who are trustworthy.

If a child cannot trust his mother, it is unlikely he will ever trust anyone else. The feeling of trust a mother establishes in her child, or fails to establish, will permeate the rest of his life.

When the one person on whom a child depends turns out to be not his protector but his chief danger, everything that happens to him looms as menace. He will grow up in terror. Fantasies of revenge will obsess him. As might be expected of the man who wrote a novel about the hero turning into a cockroach, Franz Kafka described his feelings of fear about "parents" (obviously his own) in a letter to Elli Hermann from Prague in 1921. He discussed whether parents or educators were best qualified to be entrusted with the education of children:

> *The selfishness of parents—the authentic parental emotion—knows no bounds . . . parents do not stand in a free relationship to their children. . . . When the father "educates" the child (it is the same for the mother) he will, for example, find things in the child that he already hates in himself and could not overcome and which he now hopes to overcome, since the weak child seems to be more in his power than he himself. And so in a blind fury, without waiting for the child's own development, he reaches into the depths of the growing human being to pluck out the offending element . . .*
>
> *Thus tyranny or slavery, born of selfishness, are the two educational methods of parents; all gradations of tyranny or slavery. Tyranny can express itself as great tenderness ("You must believe me, since I am your mother") and slavery can express itself as pride ("You are my son, so I will make you into my savior"). But these are two frightful educational methods, two antieducational methods, and like to trample the child back into the ground from which he came. . . . The love that parents have for their children is animal, mindless, and always prone to confuse the child with their own selves.*

The feeling of trust is never absolute—there are degrees of trust, as with all feelings. There are mothers who can be trusted by their child most of the time. There are mothers who can never be trusted. There are mothers who can be trusted a fair share of the time, emotionally enough secure to warrant their child not becoming delinquent or psychotic.

A child has to pretend to trust his mother, even though she may beat or cripple him. The battered child can hope a mother or father, though they treat him barbarically, at least will feed him and keep him alive.

Far too many children live in what the poet Lucy Larcom described as a world that is "a vale of tears." There was a heartbreaking scene in a recent television drama on the battered child when a little boy ran, with love in his eyes, to the father who had beaten him, a father who, the boy believed, loved him even though when drunk, he would again beat him severely.

Whether a mother loves her infant, hates him, or is indifferent to him, is less significant than the fact that the totality of his experience fails to meet his specific emotional needs and causes him to perceive the environment, on the whole, as an extremely frustrating one, in the words of Dr. Hyman Spotnitz, psychoanalyst.

"In any case, the child's emotional reality is that he does not feel love," explains Spotnitz. "Let us assume he correctly senses that his mother does not love him; in this situation the healthy assumption is that she lacks the capacity to do so. But the unloved child fights against admitting this to himself. He would rather believe that he is undeserving of his mother's love than that she is emotionally defective. Thus, the desirable attitude is distorted in the child's unconscious into the fiction that it is he who is defective—a bad child who is undeserving of love. If he can just stop hating, having bad thoughts and misbehaving, he can make himself over into the kind of child his mother can love. In this way, he preserves the hope of receiving love."

Humiliations in childhood that may cause loss of self-esteem are described by Karen Horney. She mentions such experiences as "being discriminated against for the sake of other children, being spurned, being treated as a plaything by the parents, being sometimes spoiled and other times shamed and snubbed." Often such experiences are forgotten because of their painful nature.

The person who, as a child, has suffered many humiliations at the hands of parents may wish to humiliate others, as was done to him. But he represses this wish, knowing how hurt and vindictive he felt when humiliated. However, his wishes may occasionally emerge without his being conscious of it, Horney says, "in an inadvertent disregard of others, such as letting them wait, in inadvertently bringing them into embarrassing situations, in letting them feel dependent."

Because such a person "cannot help registering with painful accuracy all the thousand little incidents of real life which do not fit in with his fantastic notions of his own value and importance," he wavers, Horney maintains, "in his self-valuation between feeling great and feeling worthless. At any minute he may shift from one extreme to the other. He easily feels hurt, despised, neglected, slighted and reacts with proportionate vindictive resentment."

Many men and women, because of the early lack of trust in their mothers, find it difficult to go through the mourning process because their self-esteem is already so low they defend staunchly against a further blow. They are unable to "pluck from the memory a rooted sorrow."

Most of us as children were not battered physically or abandoned by mothers. But we have had to mourn the loss inherent in separation from our mothers that is part of normal growth. This process of separation, studied by Dr. Margaret Mahler, has been named "separation-individuation." She observed how mothers and babies affect each other, with emphasis on the infant's separation.

Declaring that the death of a mother, or her physical absence, is an infrequent occurrence as compared to the widespread existence in mothers of depressive moods or depressive illness, Mahler maintains that in such cases the child's loss "is one of fantasy, that is to say *intrapsychic conflicts* of a particular type of constellation."

Every one of us as an infant has to face giving up the belief we are one with our mother, as we were inside her womb. We have to be able to bear her loss as we separate from her. We must give up the fantasy of what psychoanalysts call "symbiotic omnipotence"—the belief we and our mother are all-powerful, that no one will ever frustrate us, that we live in a magical world of pleasure, which for an infant consists of eating, sleeping, urinating and defecating at will.

As we mature physically we are expected to mature emotionally. This means we start to give up the attachment to our mother and establish our own independence and identity. But we also depend on our mother to help us in this crucial time of life, when we are most vulnerable to hurt. We expect her to function as "a protective shield," in Mahler's words.

Psychoanalysts have discovered it takes thirty-six months for an infant to feel and behave as if he had an identity of his own, not merely an extension of his mother. During this period there should exist what Mahler calls "a mutual cueing of mother and child." The child conveys to his mother his physical and emotional needs. She in turn conveys to him she has understood and will take care of him.

If a mother is incapable of understanding her child's needs, she misses his cues, failing to offer enough assurances of love and comfort. What Mahler calls "a deficit in mothering" results. This lowers a child's self-esteem and depression follows.

Mahler reports that small children who show "the basic depressive mood" do not possess much confidence or self-esteem. Too great a portion of their aggression goes into defenses that ward off rage and a fear of annihilating the mother through murderous fantasies. At the same time they struggle to restore the state of oneness with the mother, from which they should be emerging.

It is Mahler's theory that if the natural spurt to grow physically and learn to sit up, crawl and walk, as well as to think takes place in infants at the same time as a lag in their emotional readiness to function separately from the mother, the infant will feel "organismic panic."

The thoughts and fantasies with which he tries to combat the panic are not readily discernible, she says, because he is still unable to talk. His bodily growth proceeds but emotional development has been hindered, thwarted or blocked. Such severe damage may have been done that the child becomes psychotic, unable to move out of the fantasy world he has created as defense because his ego is so shattered.

Mahler found out that whereas most mothers, except the very psychotic, take care of their baby's physical needs, the capability among mothers for maintaining the infant's "basic trust" differs, both qualitatively and quantitatively, even under normal circumstances. It is easy to see, she says, that some infants have a somewhat lesser "sending power" (faulty or less cueing ability) than others. Also, some mothers are less attuned to their infant's primitive emotional needs and the child may have to overexert himself to obtain what he needs.

She maintains a child must be ready emotionally to separate from his mother in order to develop *psychically*, even though his limbs perform greater and greater tasks and he has a high I.Q. If he is not emotionally ready for the separation, he will resent it and live in fury at being forced to undertake more than he is equipped to handle. Because of his fury, he will feel guilty, then depressed. This may be the basis for later depression.

Mahler's important study shows that the small child who suffers "the basic, depressive mood" lacks enough self-confidence to master reality adequately. Too large a part of his energy is used for defenses that ward off a devastating sense of loss. These defenses hide his wish to return to a former, less painful psychic state which, to him means oneness with his mother. He will be crippled emotionally the rest of his life.

Mahler also maintains not enough emphasis has been given in the study of early depression to what she calls "the double trauma" of toilet training and the discovery (much earlier than has been generally thought) by a child of the anatomical differences between the sexes. If a child has trouble accepting the loss of the mother during the first separations, he will suffer from "the emotion-ridden symbolic significance of the phase of toilet training which follows," in which "the loss of feces is felt as a loss of part of the self."

She believes such emotional trauma as the birth of a brother or sister, if it coincides with conflicts over separation, while important, does not by itself cause depression. Rather, the birth of a rival accentuates, dramatizes and compounds "the basically negative mood predisposition of the child," she says.

In other words, it is not the birth of a rival that causes a child to feel abandoned and depressed but the degree of emotional security he has received up to that time. If he feels a sense of basic trust in his mother, he will accept all future crises without undue anxiety. To put it another way, it is not the lone "shock trauma" that harms a child but the day-by-day aura of living provided by the mother which can either cushion the occasional hurts or make them seem psychic atom bombs.

Mahler's study of how mothers relate to their infants shows what may happen if a child is unable to handle the early losses of life because he has not received enough emotional sustenance from his mother to help him separate successfully from her and achieve a sense of self-esteem. Depression and the various defenses erected to hold back his grief and anger at the loss of trust in his mother may form a pattern that will persist throughout life, as later losses stir memories of the original ones.

Mahler believes some degree of depression is a normal part of the human condition, in that a child will always feel some hate for his mother. His hatred and the ensuing guilt result in his turning aggression inward. Thus there will be grief and anger in mourning the loss of the earlier "good" mother who satisfied every need.

One woman in analysis arrived at a session tearful because a younger sister, whom she thought wholeheartedly loved and trusted her, suddenly turned on her and angrily criticized her as "dominating" and "selfish." She felt destitute emotionally, as if she had lost the love of her sister and could no longer trust her.

"I wanted to die," she said to the analyst, tears streaming down her face. "Why did she do it?"

"We don't know why," he said. "But why does her criticism seem so cataclysmic to you?"

"I feel a strange sense of déjà vu—as though I had been part of the same scene years ago," she said.

"Describe the scene," he said.

"I was about twelve and my mother turned on me suddenly, criticizing me as selfish in front of my sister, who was then nine."

"How did you feel?"

"Just as I did when my sister attacked me. That the only person in the world I loved had suddenly turned on me." She added in anger, "I *hate* my sister. The little traitor! I'll never trust her again."

"Was that how you felt about your mother?"

"I never trusted her again," she said sadly.

This woman was able eventually to face her rage at the "bad" mother, no longer the "good" mother of infancy, and at the younger sister who later reminded her of the "bad" mother.

Dr. Sandor Lorand, who has studied and treated the depressed person, finds as a rule the patient's conflicts center not only around his mother but all members of the family responsible, in his fantasy, for her loss in early childhood, though the mother is still the important person in his life.

"The patient's memory retains from the very earliest years the frustrations by the mother; it is this frustrating, threatening, punishing attitude of hers which stands out most conspicuously in the patient's recollections, overshadowing the mother's love," he says.

He adds that when a father, brothers or sisters interfere with a child's wish for sole possession of the mother's love, "an unlimited jealousy" is aroused in the child against other members of the family. This becomes responsible for the tremendous envy that is a notable characteristic of depression.

Thus hostility against the world is hostility displaced from the early years in which the "world" was mother, father, brothers and sisters, as Lorand puts it. He says it becomes clear during a patient's psychoanalysis that "the adult situation that precipitates the current depression is emotionally identical with

the patient's childhood environment.'' In the analyses of depressed men and women he found they all in childhood "had
endured experiences which caused severe infantile neuroses,
which may be looked upon as the earliest depression.''

The observations by psychoanalysts of depressed patients show it
is how a mother has accepted her losses that influences how the
child accepts his losses. A depressed mother makes her child feel
responsible for her depression, which comes across to him as
hatred—he senses the underlying hatred in depression. A child is
also naturally egocentric and imagines he is the cause of his
mother's hate. This is a burden many children bear—the psychic
impact of the mother's unmourned losses.

In growing up we have not only our own powerful passions
we must learn to control but at times the strong passions of our
mother and father with which to contend. If, as a child, we have
lived in the wake of a mother's depression, we are likely to
dramatize in later life what otherwise might not be a severe loss.
We may suffer the breaking of an unimportant date or a dinner
plate as though it were a Greek tragedy.

In a depressed atmosphere the frustrations a child must learn
to endure to become civilized may appear intolerable—the sharing of toys with brothers and sisters, control of his excretory
functions, the separations from his mother. The depressed mother
is unlikely to encourage her child, whose life begins with complete dependency, to become independent. When he is forced to
become separated from her before emotionally ready, he will hate
her with a vengeance far exceeding that of the less dependent
child.

Children at first believe their mother perfect, even though
she may be a combination of Medea, who killed two sons, and
Jocasta, who, along with her husband, King Laius, ordered her
son killed by a shepherd. Children cannot afford to risk losing a
mother's love. They may repress their anger and indulge in fantasy. If they are hungry and their mother is late with food, they
suck their thumbs, believing this will stem hunger. Or they may
urinate or defecate, thinking this less dangerous than
screaming—mothers and fathers have been known to kill a
screaming baby, so uncontrolled their rage.

We all need fantasy to survive. Dr. Martin Grotjahn writes eloquently of fantasy in childhood:

> *The greatest mental dread of a child: that he may someday lose control of his bad thoughts, and they may suddenly get loose like a swarm of bats from a cave after sunset. We live in constant dread that our unconscious may find its way to consciousness and may overwhelm our controls, then Mr. Hyde would overpower Dr. Jekyll and would do all the bad things we had hoped were safely repressed a long time ago.*

Many a child feels, "If I ever let myself go, I will destroy everyone who has ever hurt me. I will kill my mother and father, brothers and sisters." We are all afraid of the monster within— our unbridled, primitive passions, which include the desire for revenge.

A child also senses in a depressed mother her unconscious wish to murder. Some psychoanalysts have written of the effect of unspoken criminal wishes of the parent upon the behavior of a child, who may carry out what his parent unconsciously desires. Several psychoanalysts have pointed out that in the legend of Oedipus, the tragic acts were originally set in motion by his parents' attempt to kill him when he was a baby to prevent the prophecy of the Delphic oracle coming true—that he would murder his father and marry his mother.

Some children have killed parents, though this occurs more rarely than a parent killing a child. When a child kills a parent, it is reasonable to assume the child is getting even for the hatred shown him over the years.

A nineteen-year-old youth in New York City several years ago served poisoned cocktails to his mother and father because they refused to give him money to rent an apartment with a homosexual friend. A sixteen-year-old girl persuaded her boyfriend to stab her mother to death and encase her in plaster of paris in the bathtub after her mother forbade her to see the boyfriend, though the mother, divorced, had brought a succession of her own men friends to the house. A young man of eighteen shot and killed his mother, father and two brothers because, he said, his father insisted he return to a military school he hated.

Another kind of loss of trust in a parent occurs if a child is seduced by a parent. When the parent, supposed to be the protector, assaults the body and emotions of the child, he breaks society's strongest taboo. Roger O. Olive, chief psychologist at the Ionia State Hospital in Michigan, reports incest occurs in one out of each one thousand persons, that "one out of every ten children seen at community child-care facilities is involved in incestuous behavior." Physicians are usually reluctant to report such cases for fear of harming the child further and because it is difficult for them to believe parents could inflict such indignity on children.

When a child loses one or both parents and never finds a loving substitute, his unexpressed grief and rage may cause tragic consequences in later life, like the suicide of Marilyn Monroe (whether deliberate or "accidental" does not matter). In spite of beauty, fame and wealth, she never recovered from the losses of her early life. She did not know her father and as a child was sent by her emotionally disturbed mother to foster homes, where she received little love. Nothing could make up for the early losses she was unable to mourn successfully.

Since children in their first years of life depend on parents to nourish their self-esteem, to be motherless, fatherless, an orphan or adopted is felt by a child as "utterly degrading," according to Dr. Edith Jacobson, who has studied the nature of loss and depression. She says children experience the loss of a parent not only in terms of loss of love "but also as a severe narcissistic injury, a castration." As Freud said, our first ego is a "body ego" and a loss threatens the physical image of ourselves.

Jacobson reports that men and women who in early childhood have lost one or both parents "show the emotional scars left by their infantile psychic injury. In most of them the old wounds have never healed." Their ability to relate to others is seriously impaired. They suffer depression and other symptoms in which the traumatic experiences of infancy play a decisive role.

When one parent dies or leaves the home, the child's hostility becomes directed at the parent who remains, Jacobson says. She explains:

The fact that in such children the hostile and derogatory feelings caused by their losses are so commonly diverted to the surviving parent or the parent substitutes, while the lost object becomes glorified, tends to raise that object's narcissistic value and meaning to the point of turning it into the most precious part of the self which has been lost and must be recovered.

Jacobson advances the theory that too early a disappointment, or loss of faith in parents, will cause depression. She describes "disappointment" as an experience that occurs when promises and expectations of gratification are not fulfilled. She states that oral frustration, in particular a state of severe and lasting hunger, seems to be the earlier forerunner of profound disappointment "such as comes about later by being hit by the loss of a most valuable object." If a mother fails to feed a hungry baby on time, the baby will become depressed. In later life, a minor disappointment may revive this feeling of severe depression, "the feeling of blank, empty hopelessness, of nothingness, often accompanied by the sensation of physical emptiness."

As every infant grows and learns to think for himself, a process of disillusionment sets in, caused by increasing disappointments inflicted by the mother and father as they attempt to civilize the child. These disappointments force the child "to a critical revision of the illusionary parental images," says Jacobson. Whether this process of disillusionment has a constructive or destructive effect on the development of the child's ego and his sense of reality "depends less on the severity of the disappointments in the parents than on the stage at which they set in."

The child who has been disappointed too early cannot use his disillusionment for the development of his self-respect. On the contrary, he "must get involved in the collapse of his world of magic," in Jacobson's words. Instead of acquiring a realistic picture of the world, the child may swing from an optimistic to a pessimistic illusion which distorts reality.

"The parents, once omnipotent gods, as they pass through the grid of devaluating criticism, may turn into bad, hostile, punishing beings not only deprived of their divine power but appearing bad in a deprecatory way; low, defiled, empty, castrated . . . evil as well as worthless," she says.

As the ego of the infant takes part in the downfall of the

godlike parents, their destruction becomes identical with self-deflation and self-destruction. The child will respond, from then on, to any disappointment with a narcissistic hurt. He will also become sensitized for direct attacks on his narcissism or for failure to adjust to the world. He will react to attacks as to disappointments inflicted by someone he loves.

This creates an interaction of disappointment and narcissistic injury causing and affecting each other, whose beginnings one can observe in connection with cleanliness training. Jacobson cites the instance of a thirty-six-year-old writer whose earliest recollection of a depression led back to the age of three.

He recalled being in the bathroom, sitting on "a chamber pot," feeling alone and remote from his mother. She was taking care of the other children, particularly his next older brother, her pet. Eventually, she turned to him, lifted him from the pot, looked in and said derogatorily, "Nothing of course."

His older brother had smiled at his humiliation. He remembered vividly the dull, empty, desperate hopelessness connected with the feeling of utter worthlessness, typical of this time of his life and of his later depressions. On the surface this scene seemed to revolve around the rejection by his mother because of her son's failure to "produce," Jacobson comments. But in his analysis, the man's stubborn refusal to "produce" was repeated in his writing and sexual relationships with women, and represented a "vindictive and at the same time masochistic response to his mother's neglect." Jacobson summed up, "Since she [his mother] does not care for him, he cannot give her anything. As she appears worthless to him, his anal present loses its value and becomes dirt. The ensuing rejection on her part crushes the infantile ego all the more and causes further disappointment, so that a vicious circle arises."

Severe disillusionment in the parents during the first years of life "crushes" the infantile ego on the one hand, and, on the other, may start the formation of conscience at an earlier stage than usual, Jacobson asserts.

Thus psychoanalysts discovered the earlier in life a child experiences physical or psychic cruelty at the hands of a

*parent, the more "lost" he will feel, the more severe will be
the impact of future losses and the less self-esteem he will
possess.*

*This explains why some mourn a loss and are done
with it, whereas others sink into a depression that may last
for years. Depression, when deep, starts not with any loss
of later life, though such a loss may spark it, but in childhood. Its roots lie in infancy, perhaps even in the womb.
Research at the Fels Institute shows that if a pregnant
woman is depressed this affects the physical and emotional
reactions of the fetus.*

The "demons" and "voices" in the mind of the psychotic represent the lost loved/hated mother who still "possesses" him emotionally, from whom he has been unable to separate. When David
Berkowitz spoke of "demons" within that urged him to kill, the
demons stood for his own murderous impulses but also referred to
his natural mother, who gave him up at birth, and his foster
mother, who died of cancer when he was fourteen (we can imagine the impact upon him, as a boy, of her depression during the
years she was dying). The measure of his self-esteem may be
gauged by his reference to himself as a "dog" and "less than
human," how he must have felt as a child. If ever he were to
speak of his feelings to a psychoanalyst, we might get a glimpse
of the infant rage that drove him to vicious murders of the innocent.

How angry we become as a child depends mainly on two
things, according to psychological experts: the quality of care
given by our mother—influenced by whether she is fearful, depressed, impatient or ignorant of our needs—and our capacity to
accept delay, tolerate frustration. Both the quality of our mother's
care and our capacity to accept frustration set an emotional tone
that pervades our life and influences how we face our losses.

Though childhood may be remembered as a time of innocence and happiness, no period in life compares to it in the
number of losses and the intensity of day-by-day disappointments.

"As a period of disappointment and renunciation childhood

has no parallel, nor is there a richer source of frustration, unrequited wishes, or expectations that fail,'' says Dr. Gregory Rochlin, psychoanalyst.

The child ''is obliged to repress his deepest emotions, often those of love and usually hate, give up many pleasurable achievements, give up wanting his own way, believing his every wish should be fulfilled,'' explains Rochlin. ''It is then his defenses arise, defenses that remain with him throughout life.''

We will always hold within us some sense of mourning for the lost pleasures of infancy. But as we can accept the losses of the past, we find more appropriate pleasures.

We will not need to resort to addiction of any kind to relieve our pain at a loss. We will seek a suitable substitute for our first lost love, even though we never fully give her up.

5

The Rewards of Loss

We do not live in Utopia where "all losses are restor'd and sorrows end," as Shakespeare wrote in Sonnet 30. But out of our losses can come high rewards as well as grief, anger and a sense of deprivation.

For the natural conclusion to mourning is the seeking of restitution. Which means the mourning process, when fulfilled, becomes a way to growth. We mourn someone or something lost, to whom or to which we have had a deep attachment, and through the mourning we feel new strength to find a satisfactory replacement. Proust put it, "It is grief that develops the powers of the mind."

Restitution for our losses starts early in life. As a baby, we believe we have lost our mother when she vanishes, not knowing her absence is only temporary. We use our imagination to envision her face, as though this will restore her.

A child who feels deserted when his mother leaves the house to go shopping may seek restitution for his loss by transferring his love and feelings of loss to a pet. One little boy patted his puppy on the head and said, "You miss your mommy, don't you?" The play *Harvey*, by Mary Chase, in which the imaginary six-foot rabbit becomes the hero's best friend, is eloquent example of how one man tried to make restitution for an early loss, in either fact or fantasy, of a loved/hated mother.

A child who breaks a toy demands of its mother or father, "Fix it!" and waits impatiently for the toy, lost to use, to be restored. One of the most pleasurable games of childhood is the hiding of an object, or the self, by one child as others eagerly look for the lost object or child.

Far from being a time of anguish, in spite of losses childhood "is filled with hope; the drive toward fulfillment does not abate," in the words of Dr. Rochlin. He maintains losses strewn through childhood are recouped by restitution.

Our entire emotional development may be seen, he says, as filled with movement from one phase to the next, "each one driven by its characteristic repudiations, restrictions and limitations, and forging on toward the next phase, with restitution taking place in each phase."

What we renounce in one developmental period we may regain in another form in the next, in the course of which mastery over our instincts is won, Rochlin says. As our forbidden wishes—to kill a rival, to have erotic pleasure with our mother or father, to masturbate at will—give way to incomplete rewards, a repository of these prohibited wishes remains in our unconscious. Restitution is always being sought for these lost wishes, frequently through sublimation. Rochlin explains:

> *At each level of psychic development something of pleasure is relinquished and then through restitution is regained. Thus an enormous impetus to extend one's limits is supplied by what is relinquished. The effort to gain something pleasurable that is lost, or a valued object, or to reinstate a*

*tarnished self-esteem makes possible a rich variety of substi-
tute gratifications.*

If someone is too emotionally impoverished to reach for a substitute, insisting on regaining exactly what is lost, unable to tolerate
a change, he is likely to face lengthy suffering, warns Rochlin.

One of the ways our mind helps us make restitution for
present and past losses is through dreams. A dream pictures the
disguised fulfillment of a wish that has been repressed because
we believe it dangerous to self-esteem. Rochlin calls dreams ''an
essential part of the lifelong cycle of losses and restitution.''

Someone snubs us at a party. We feel furious but repress the
feeling. That night we dream we are a king who orders a person,
vaguely resembling the one who has snubbed us, to be beheaded.
We get revenge in fantasy, saved from a guilty conscience, for
it's only a dream.

One overweight woman was put on a strict diet by her
doctor and ordered to give up her cherished desserts. Starved
most of the day, she found her dreams overflowing with images
of luscious chocolate cakes and candies, mounds of all flavors of
ice cream topped with fudge and butterscotch sauces, fulfilling in
fantasy her frustrated wishes.

Telling a friend of her dreams, she said, ''They fill my mind
if not my empty stomach and they don't make me fat!''

Why is it so difficult to accept a loss? Rochlin says: ''To do
so means to give up the demands for imperishable relationships,
to acknowledge the transience of all things without resort to denial and without a counter-belief in immortality, to renounce
expectations of wishing to alter reality, and hence to give up wish
fulfillment.''

Placing a high value on another person makes it difficult to
accept a substitute. A part of the self has been transferred to that
person, invested in the qualities valued in him. With the loss of
that person, the part of the self given over vanishes (the sense of
emptiness felt after a loss).

There is not a loss in childhood, not a repression of grief and
anger that follows on a loss, but that our emotional balance becomes upset and we attempt to restore it.

The degree and duration of a child's dependence on another person to reach and maintain this psychic balance has no parallel in other animals, Rochlin points out. He says: "The attempt to attain a corrective equilibrium of gratifications is an essential part of human emotional development, but the modification of the basic gap between what is demanded and what is satisfied are only possible through the help of another person."

That other person is the mother. If a mother's care is overprotective and dominating, or if she neglects the child's needs, she encourages dependence, not independence. Her child's efforts to master his losses will be feeble and inadequate.

A child who, in reality, loses his mother early in life will suffer far more than one whose mother is present, unless the first child is fortunate enough to gain a mother substitute who understands his loss and genuinely cares for him. Rochlin believes, though some psychoanalysts disagree, that in the earliest months of life, when self-interest is at its height, the child easily accepts a substitute for the mother. As the child's interest in others develops and deepens, "the substitution of one person for another is correspondingly more difficult to achieve." Rochlin says: "An intimate concern with another person correspondingly reduces the readiness to accept a substitute for that person."

The discovery that losses start early in life and have a profound effect on our emotions led Rochlin to originate the phrase "the loss complex." He explains: "The loss of a loved one in childhood, whether in fact or fancy, produces a highly organized galaxy of sequential psychic phenomena which are best understood as a loss complex." He has written a book, *Griefs and Discontents: The Forces of Change*, elaborating on this idea.

The loss of a loved one "in fact or fancy" refers not only to a mother's absence or death but the loss suffered by a child when, for instance, his mother speaks sharply or punishes him.

A four-year-old girl who stamped her foot and screamed at her mother, "I won't!" when ordered to put on rubbers if she wanted to go out in the rain, felt hurt when her mother said, "You won't get dessert tonight for talking to me in that tone of voice."

The mother kept her threat. The little girl burst into tears at the dinner table. This was the first time she had been punished so severely and she thought she had lost her mother's love. She could not control her grief.

A child feels loss of his mother's love when she bears another baby or leaves him at a time he needs her. He feels a deep sense of loss when he first learns the meaning of death and realizes he too will lose his life someday.

A father took his five-year-old daughter to the aquarium for a Sunday afternoon's outing. They passed one tank of tropical fishes in which a large fish had died and lay inert at the bottom. The little girl stared at it in horror.

Her father said gently, "The fish won't hurt you. It's dead."

"Is that what dead is?" she asked.

"Yes," said the father, adding reassuringly, "It was a very old fish. It lived a long, happy life."

The little girl shuddered, said, "Let's get out of here," and seemed preoccupied the rest of the afternoon. Her father realized this was her first experience with death. She had become aware that if animals could die, so could she.

During the early years, the fear of loss, the dread of abandonment and the thought of dying constitute "our three major conflicts," according to Rochlin. Each conflict acts "in concert with the others as the loss complex."

These conflicts, he adds, are based on the three convictions: relationships are tentative, that is, not permanent; stability is threatened by change from within and outside the self; and there exists a deep and necessary dependence on others.

Losses—and griefs and small mournings—are "part of the everyday attitudes of childhood," Rochlin observes, as well as accompanying the natural traumas of psychosexual development, such as weaning and toilet training.

During the third, or phallic, phase of psychosexual development, the child becomes aware his erotic wishes for the parent of the opposite sex will never be fulfilled, that he has forever lost this passionate love. It is a "colossal love," according to Rochlin, and with it, "the *loss complex*" is firmly rooted.

Both the repression of Oedipal wishes and the repression of feelings connected to losses help develop the ego—"the engine of change at work," in Rochlin's words, as we acquire strong defenses against our erotic and aggressive wishes.

The child, as he suffers a loss, has to learn to cope with his strong inner impulses of hostility. He pays for the security of his parents' protection, ensuring their love, by repressing impulses of hate.

A boy of four becomes infuriated when his two-year-old sister snatches his favorite toy, a giraffe, out of his hands. His impulse is to hit her and take back the giraffe. But his mother is watching and he knows he will be punished, fears he will be hated, if he strikes his little sister. So he smiles wanly and pretends to feel no anger. He goes to his paint box and colors a picture of a brown and white cow grazing in a green field. He is learning to sublimate his anger in some creative way. Instead of giving in to an urge to destroy another human, he uses his energy to enhance the world.

Children also have to learn that life is not governed by magic, that to wish for something does not mean it automatically happens. A little girl of five, seeing a baby brother brought into the house from the hospital, wished he would disappear forever. A week later the infant boy died of pneumonia. The little girl believed she killed him because of her wish. Her belief in magic—the power of her wishes—plus her intense jealousy, for which she felt guilty, convinced her she caused his death.

Each phase of our psychosexual development—oral, anal, phallic and genital—contains strong demands for gratification of sexual and aggressive wishes. If our emotional development is to take place naturally, we have to learn to accept frustration and modification of these demands, helped by warm, loving parents. Our ability to accept a loss and make restitution, such as the giving of love to someone else or sublimating grief in work, depends on the kind of relationship we have had in early life with our mother.

The relationship to a mother will always hold a certain amount of ambivalence—we hate her for frustrating us and for abandoning us at times of need. Rochlin notes that after a parent's death a child's identification with the parent intensifies, for the child does not want to let go of what he has lost. Death intensifies the hate aspect of ambivalence as well as the love, he adds.

The wish to restore what we have lost or given up, as well as to transcend our limits ("Ah, but a man's reach should exceed his grasp," as Browning said), goes on until we die. The process of restitution is a continuous one. If restitution is not sought, depression persists.

One woman, after her husband's death, became so depressed she could not move out of the house. She lost twenty pounds because she refused to eat. Then she decided she would no longer give in to such self-pity. She made up her mind to study fashion designing, put to practical use her interest in clothes. She took courses, her sketches were praised by instructors and within two years she was hired by a New York manufacturer to design dresses. She was able to change a destructive attitude into a constructive one as she sought restitution.

Whether efforts at restitution are infantile or mature is dictated by whether the aims are "childish or adult," says Rochlin. If the experience of loss merely leads to attempts at "simple restoration," there will be little psychological change or emotional fulfillment.

One woman of thirty-five, when her marriage broke up, felt inconsolable. She could not sleep, eat or hold back tears until she found a man who comforted her with caresses and sexual climaxes, then held her close as she slept.

The affair did not last, so she embarked on another, and another. Finally she went into analysis, ashamed of such wanton behavior.

She said to her analyst, "Unless I have sex, I feel I will die."

"If you do, it will be the first case on record," he said.

"Why do I feel so desperate?" she asked.

"You are suffering the loss of your husband."

"But I don't even *like* him anymore," she protested.

"That's part of your desperate feeling—you are guilty because of your repressed anger at him."

During the analysis she discovered her anger at her husband

had masked fury at a father who had indulged in affairs, never hiding them from his family. She had unconsciously imitated his way of coping with what he had felt as a loss—loss of love for his wife.

Such restitution brings little happiness beyond the momentary release of tension. This woman realized she had to stop the promiscuity and understand her deeper feelings. She eventually married another man, this time making a wiser choice.

Usually a loss forces substitutions and sublimations, plays a critical role in emotional development and tests our measure of achievement, according to Rochlin. He quotes Freud:

"Really we never can relinquish anything; we only exchange one thing for something else. When we appear to give something up, all we really do is to adopt a substitute."

With each loss comes the impulse for restitution. This impulse is unconscious—we cannot will it or hold it back. If we lose an article, or it is stolen from us, we automatically wish to replace it with a similar one. If we cannot find restitution, we become grief-stricken.

Grief is not the same as sadness. Sadness follows the loss of a loved one or object, either real, threatened or fantasied, but not a giving up. In sadness there is nostalgia, longing and hope for eventual reunion, though the image of the self is felt in varying degrees to be impoverished, deprived, empty, weakened or in some way deficient, according to Dr. G. L. Engel. He believes there is a continuum, with sadness at one end of the spectrum and despair at the other.

Instead of restitution there may be regression. This means the mourning process is incomplete, the person has not found "a time to mourn," as the Bible advises. He may instead try to drown his sorrow in drink or take to drugs. Or wallow in promiscuity. Or become apathetic, lose all initiative. There are many ways to deny grief and rage.

In describing regression Freud compared it to an advancing army suddenly faced with a strong enemy and forced to retreat to more secure defensive positions—to points of earlier fixation. Dr. Lawrence J. Friedman expands this thought:

"When we retreat in the hope of avoiding sudden danger, we give up the terrain; we retreat to a position better known to us, but the conflict is not solved. The battle continues. We retreat, but the enemy follows. The difference is that we are now fighting on a different terrain, under different conditions."

He uses as example the person who reaches the Oedipal conflict but is incapable of dealing with it. Earlier conflicts on the oral and anal levels become reactivated as there is regression from the phallic stage, first to the previous anal stage. "This anality will give us a picture similar to, but not identical with, the previous anality," Friedman explains. "It is, so to speak, soaked through with Oedipal elements. Instead of achieving its goal, namely, avoidance of the Oedipus complex, the regression has made the situation worse. Now gratification, as well as successful defences against anal drives, such as sublimation, become untenable. Now genitality is inevitably connected with aggression, for aggression is part of every anality.

"The same situation is inevitable if the regression goes further back to orality. Now the Oedipus complex influences the orality to such an extent that successful defences against oral drives become impossible. Castration anxiety no longer looks like castration anxiety but the fear of being eaten, the fear of losing love, the fear of starvation. But it still means castration anxiety, which in the original orality was non-existent."

He cites an old Viennese joke as illustrative of what happens. At one time in Vienna it was difficult for a Jew to achieve a high position professionally or socially. Frequently, to surmount this obstacle, Jews became converted to Catholicism, the official religion of Austria. One Jewish family, aspiring to high social status, accepted the conversion and sent their son, who spoke with a decided Jewish accent, to a Catholic convent so he would lose his accent. After he had been there a year, the parents visited him. They found not that the little boy had lost his Jewish accent but everyone in the convent had acquired one.

"There is a parallel situation in the retreat from the Oedipus complex," Friedman says. "The Oedipus complex follows the retreat to the new terrain but instead of being defeated, it colours everything. It influences the former orality to such an extent that the orality speaks the Oedipal language. Now we see that primal scene phantasies are connected with oral destructive phantasies. Oedipal longing is expressed in longing for warmth and affection, in insatiable hunger, in the need for an ever-flowing, abundant breast; castration anxiety is expressed as fear of starvation. Yet we have only to listen: slips of the tongue, dreams, phantasies will show us clearly that this orality is a hiding place for the Oedipus complex, sometimes well concealed, sometimes only thinly veiled.''

But most of us resort to restitution, not regression, after passing through the early stages of the mourning process. If we feel we suffer too deeply from losses, unable to find a new love or to put energy into achieving new fulfillments, we may wish to seek help to become aware of our hidden grief and anger.

Becoming creative is one rewarding way of gaining restitution for a loss. How is the creative process connected to losses and mourning?

6
Combating Loss Through Creativity

The discovery that a loss is accompanied by the wish to restore what is lost, often by re-creating it in fantasy, led to new understanding of the nature of creativity which has long puzzled mankind.

When we lose someone we love, one of our first wishes is to bring the person back. Our unconscious never gives up on a wish and one of the ways it devises to regain the lost loved one is to restore him symbolically as long as he cannot be restored realistically.

In an attempt at restoration and reparation, a man or woman of genius may paint a work of art, compose a symphony, write a novel. Michelangelo and Leonardo da Vinci both lost their mothers at a very early age. At birth Michelangelo was given to a foster family. Leonardo, an illegitimate baby, was taken from his peasant mother before the age of five by his wealthy father, who had married a woman in his social class. These two geniuses spent their lives seeking to restore "the loved object" in a creative way, building lasting memorials of beauty in tribute to their lost love.

Possibly one of the most depressed writers ever to live was Dostoevski, who in fiction described many of his losses, conflicts and fantasies, including the wish to murder, in *Crime and Punishment*, and his obsessive need to gamble, in *The Gambler*.

Edgar Allan Poe is another whose life held a series of losses. His mother died when he was a child, then later, his young wife. His short stories hold the murderous wishes he must have felt, mourning unfulfilled. His excessive drinking and drug addiction were also signs of inability to complete the mourning process.

Losses may lead the creative mind into "lonely areas that have not previously been explored by others," according to Dr. Heinz Kohut. He says: "The sense of isolation of the creative mind is both exhilarating and frightening, the latter because the experience repeats traumatically an early childhood fear of being alone, abandoned, unsupported."

The artist, musician or writer, or the statesman who achieves the greatness of a Lincoln, manages somehow to surmount the repressed grief and anger of his losses. He has the ability to put his energy in the highest form of what Freud called sublimation. This is the psychic process we use to direct sexual and aggressive energy into behavior that benefits ourselves and society.

Freud raised the question: What makes the artist able to "carry us with him in such a way and to arouse emotions in us of which we thought ourselves perhaps not even capable"?

He suggests the artist is a person of "special gifts" who has a "flexibility of repressions." This flexibility allows him to project his inner turmoil on whatever he creates so an audience can take part in the artistic experience. The flexibility also allows the energy bound up in repression to be freed. The artist, like everyone else, experiences what Freud called "the return of the repressed" but with one difference—for the purpose of glorifying life, not giving in to impulses in a destructive way. Freud wrote:

> *The artist is originally a man who turns from reality because he cannot come to terms with the demand for renunciations of instinctual satisfaction as it is first made, and who then in fantasy life allows full play to his erotic and ambitious wishes. But he finds a way of return from this world of fantasy back to reality; with his special gifts he moulds his fantasies into a new kind of reality, and men concede them a justification as valuable reflections of actual life.*

An artist presents his unconscious wishes and fantasies aesthetically so they do not arouse fear, anger or shame in those who see his productions. He puts the viewers in a position "in which we can enjoy our own day-dreams without reproach or shame," according to Freud. The aesthetic pleasure we gain from the works of imaginative writers is similar to the "fore-pleasure" of sex, and "the true enjoyment of literature proceeds from the release of tensions in our minds."

The choice of a specific sublimation, such as creativity, depends, Freud said, on what he called overdetermination—several or many early important emotional experiences. In his later years Freud attributed to the aggressive instinct a power equal to the sexual, so the aggressive or hostile urge was now also present in sublimation.

The artist is thus seen by psychoanalysts as re-creating in fantasy both the "bad" mother his hostility destroyed in his imagination and the "good" mother he loved. It is the urge to make reparation for destructive feelings that in part drives the artist, according to Dr. Melanie Klein.

She describes this urge as belonging to "the depressive position" in the life of infants. Noted for intensive psychoanalytic investigation of the very early stages of infancy, Klein became impressed with the power, and what she said might often be "the terror," of fantasy. She described fantasy as "the psychic representative of instinct." She held there was no impulse, no instinctual urge or response, that was not experienced in the mind as a fantasy. The fantasy represented the specific content of the urge or feeling dominating the mind at the moment.

After studying infants, she concluded there were two "positions" that occurred in the first years of life. She used the term "position" rather than "stage of development," she said, to emphasize "the coexistence of feelings in the earlier stage with those of the later one, rather than a complete move from a first stage into a second."

The first "position," occurring during the first six months of life, she called the paranoid-schizoid position. The second, she named the depressive position. They are both part of normal development and influence later behavior, she held.

The first position occurs when an infant, frustrated in getting what he wants—milk, a change of diapers, a warm blanket—imagines his mother is deliberately persecuting him. He does not as yet possess enough reason to figure out she may be delayed by household chores or too tired to attend promptly to his needs. His feeling is one of persecution, followed by hate. Later paranoid delusions are caused by these early feelings. A man's fantasy that some unknown enemy wishes to poison him goes back to his fantasy as a baby that his mother was trying to poison him. If a mother strongly resents having a baby, her anger may be communicated to the baby at her breast. She may feed him as though she hated keeping him alive and he may feel "poisoned" not by the milk itself but by her hate, as food and hate forever become inseparable in his mind.

Following the paranoid position, at the end of the first year of life the depressive position occurs. The infant for the first time experiences the loss of his mother, now seen as a whole person. He is aware of how it feels to lose another human being. Before that, his mother has been just a breast or warm arms holding a bottle. He has also, by now, developed a conscience, so when he becomes angry at his mother for deserting him when he needs her, he feels guilty, then depressed. This depressive position is the fount of all later depression, according to Klein.

During the earliest months of our lives, the wish to kill when we feel angry is not expressed as the wish to murder that adults feel, but as the wish to devour, to bite, or chew up, for the mouth is then all we know as weapon. When we reach the anal stage, we think of destroying someone in terms of degrading, soiling or shaming ("piss on you" or "shit on you"). When we reach the genital stage, we think of destruction in terms of actual murder—shooting, strangling, knifing.

Klein believed the depressive position was evidence of mourning the loss of the mother's breast "and all that the breast and the milk have come to stand for in the infant's mind: namely, love, goodness and security. All these are felt by the baby to be lost, and lost as a result of his own uncontrollable, greedy and destructive phantasies and impulses against his mother's breasts."

The circle of loved objects attacked in fantasy, and whose loss is therefore feared, widens as the child comes to know mixed feelings of love and hate for his father and either actual brothers and sisters or fantasied brothers and sisters inside the mother's body, Klein maintained. She said:

The increase of love and trust and the diminishing of fears through happy experiences, help the baby, step by step, to overcome his depression and feeling of loss (mourning). They enable him to test his inner reality by means of outer reality. Through being loved and through the enjoyment and comfort he has in relation to people, his confidence in his own as well as in other people's goodness becomes strengthened, his hope that his "good" objects and his own ego can be saved and preserved increases, at the same time as his ambivalence and acute fears of internal destruction diminish.

The depressive position, according to Dr. D. W. Winnicott, is "*an achievement*" (italics his) in emotional development which a number of people never attain. He calls it "a gradually strengthening evidence of personal growth that is dependent on sensitive and continual environmental provision."

He maintains that if the depressive position has been achieved and fully established, "the reaction to loss is *grief* or *sadness*" (italics his). But where there is some degree of failure in achieving the depressive position, "the result of loss is depression."

The causes of creativity are still a mystery to psychoanalysts though they are exploring them. People who create are described by Dr. Phyllis Greenacre as having "a love affair with the world." Feeling they have irreparably lost the mother of infancy they seek the love of millions to take the place of one.

Dr. Minna Emch noted that creativity seemed to occur when "exaltation" rather than depression was the main mood of infancy. She also thought creative people were sexually precocious as children and found outlet for their heightened sexual impulses through the fantasy that appeared in their creative work.

We honor the creative person because we know how difficult it is for man to sublimate his savage drives creatively. It is the highest of achievement to channel mad fantasy into a sane form of beauty that enhances life.

The successful completion of the mourning process may result in a creative outcome, as Pollock stated. He says:

> *This end result can be a great work of art, music, sculpture, literature, poetry, philosophy or science, where the creator has the spark of genius or talent that is not related to mourning* per se. *Indeed the creative product may reflect the mourning process in theme, style, form, content and it may itself stand as a memorial. In the less gifted, a creative outcome may be manifested in a new real relationship, the ability to feel joy, satisfaction, a sense of accomplishment or newer sublimations that reflect a successful resolution of the mourning process.*

Pollock cites as example of the successful completion of a mourning process the revolutionary discoveries of Freud. Immediately after his father's death Freud wrote *The Interpretation of Dreams*, the first man to discover the way to the understanding of the unconscious. Freud said he recognized the connection with his father's death only after finishing the book: "It revealed itself to me as a piece of my self analysis, as my reaction to my father's death; that is, to the most important event, the most poignant loss, in a man's life.''

Creativity may also be, Pollock says, not the outcome of a successfully completed mourning process but an attempt to complete the mourning work. Or evidence the mourning process is "grossly distorted or arrested.'' The creative attempts "may not always be successful in terms of mourning work solutions'' but the "intrinsic aesthetic or scientific merit of the work still may be great despite the failure of mourning completion.'' A successful mourning process, in other words, has to be distinguished from attempts to defend against the impact of the loss.

At times the mourning may be pathological, with a suicidal outcome, Pollock points out, citing Virginia Woolf, Anne Sexton, Sylvia Plath and John Berryman.

Dr. Hannah Segal, who described writing for Proust as his work of mourning, believes "all creation is really a re-creation of a once loved and once whole, but now lost and ruined object, a ruined internal world and self. It is when the world within us is destroyed, when it is dead and loveless, when our loved ones are in fragments, and when we ourselves are in helpless despair—it is then that we must re-create our world anew, reassemble the pieces, infuse life into dead fragments, re-create life.''

Describing creativity as "a continuation of mourning work,'' Dr. Tor-Björn Hägglund says that if, however, "creativity replaces mourning work, it is manifested in compulsory repetition,'' as when an artist paints the same image over and over or a writer's books all focus on the same plot.

Creative people who have been psychoanalyzed do not lose their creativity but their depression. The psychoanalyst helps them through the mourning process so they can accept the early losses. Their creativity is in no way diminished. What *is* diminished is the depression that has blocked full creativity.

One successful writer of fiction realized even as he sat down at the typewriter he felt irritated, impatient. He suffered as he wrote. The minute he was finished with a book, he could not wait to start another even though he knew the agony would start all over. His wife, who found him increasingly difficult to live with, convinced him to see a therapist.

During therapy he realized he had transferred much of his inner misery over past losses to his writing. He was trying to solve conflicts through his art rather than face them consciously. As he became aware of grief and anger at his losses, he discovered he now enjoyed both the planning of a book and the writing of it.

His wife told a friend, "And he's also fun around the house when he's through with his day's work. The old sourpuss has disappeared."

Some creative persons have been destroyed by their depression. Jackson Pollock, the artist, at the wheel of his car when it crashed into a tree, killing himself and a companion, and Thomas Heggen, the author of *Mister Roberts*, who committed suicide, were two. Their success did not bring release from the repressed feelings of grief and anger at childhood losses. Rage at the mother of childhood was so intense that after they re-created the loved lost one in fantasy through works of art, they killed themselves, turning inward the wish of infancy to destroy the loved/ hated mother.

The creative urge appears to be the result of a number of factors in a life. The creative person possesses what Freud called "special gifts." One of them perhaps is a sensitivity in infancy to a mother, or a mother substitute as, in Michelangelo's case his foster mother, who is responsive and loving. As a child, the creative person received enough love and approval so he could combat his losses in restorative rather than destructive fashion.

In some way, his mother or father or both, made it known he was loved for what he produced. He wished to keep on producing to hold their love. A gifted child who receives little love may not be able to use his energy to create because he needs most of it to keep his hatred repressed.

Dr. Greenacre believes "a critical situation in infancy" may contribute to creativity. A gifted child, forced to exert control of his bowels, may more readily and extensively than other children play with mud or clay as fecal substitutes, which he begins to mould according to his imaginative fantasies. "Skill in a gifted individual is but part of the unfolding of the imagination which may originally gain impetus in connection with masturbatory activity but becomes liberated from it," says Greenacre.

Declaring "the experience of awe in childhood" is often mentioned by creative persons, she speculates they may have had an early image of the father as godlike, a "penis awe." She also suggests the infancy of the gifted person holds an early and marked sensitivity to the sensory stimulation from the mother's breast, to which the gifted infant reacts "with an intensity of the impression of warmth, smell, moisture, the feel of the texture of the skin and the vision of the roundness of the form."

A large number of creative persons and overachievers in the business and professional worlds have been the oldest child. Freud believed mothers were joined to their firstborn by a special protective link. When a patient, the mother of a little boy, told Freud a frightening dream had awakened her at the last moment so she could save her child from suffocation by the bed sheets, Freud remarked, "Why do you wonder? The umbilical cord between the mother and her first-born can never be severed." He was a firstborn, attributing his self-confidence throughout life to his mother's special love.

One reason for the success, creative and otherwise, of the firstborn, may be that the sense of loss of the mother is apt to be deepest in the oldest child. He is the only one to have had her complete love in the earliest months of life. The birth of a rival may thus be more devastating to the oldest child than to those who come into the world already sharing a mother's love. When the oldest child realizes he no longer is the sole recipient of his mother's love, he feels "the mighty have fallen." His creativity, or overachievement, may be an attempt to regain his early throne as he sublimates sexual and aggressive urges. He is a rebel with artistic cause, so to speak.

Jacques Casanova was the oldest child of a mother and father who were actors and who, when he was only eighteen months, left him for three years in Venice in the care of his maternal grandmother, while they played on the stage in London. When his mother returned, she brought as rival a younger son, compounding Casanova's loss. While he became chiefly known as the world's greatest lover (caricaturing the promiscuous life both his mother and father were known to have led), he also gave the world a creative gift in his *Memoirs*, which describe eloquently not only his affairs but the economic and social life of

Europe, particularly the tyranny of Church and State, just before the French Revolution.

Though all of us cannot be a Melville or a Michelangelo we can seek restitution through creativity. With the resolution of the mourning process may come a creative outlet, according to Dr. Pollock. He has studied fourteen hundred writers, political figures, artists, sculptors and musicians and found their achievements related to mourning. The gifted men and women after a loss often use their creativity.

If, following a loss we can discover some art or interest to pursue, we will find emotional rewards. The creative spirit lies in all of us, whether or not we use it to full advantage.

A sixty-four-year-old woman, after she lost a husband to whom she had been close for forty-five years, decided to study painting. She went to art classes, worked on canvases in her home. While no Grandma Moses, she painted with such skill her friends persuaded her to sell an occasional painting. Her self-esteem rose because of the admiration of friends and family for what she had created.

Another woman, after the loss of her mother, became a successful interior decorator. Still another opened a boutique, something she had wanted to do for years. Others, following a loss, have learned photography, formed a music group, fashioned jewelry, become real-estate brokers, opened flower shops. One woman joined a Wall Street firm. Another wrote a Broadway play.

These persons all possessed the courage to master the emotional pain caused by losses. They found a way to conquer their grief and rage so they enhanced not only the world but their self-esteem. They engaged in a struggle with their primitive feelings as we all do, every day of our lives, and came out the victor.

They were able to complete the mourning process by seeking a restitution that brought pleasure. They changed their loss into a gain, proving Emerson's point that "nothing can bring you peace but yourself."

7
Overcoming Loss With Laughter

There are many ways of denying grief and anger at a loss. A manic spirit is one. But it is a way society greets with far more approval than it does depression. We enjoy laughter. We flee those who are depressed.

When we feel elated, we are "in high spirits, proud and happy, joyful," according to Webster's New World Dictionary. We look on ourselves with esteem and on the world with peaceful, friendly eyes, anger and acrimony out of mind. But if elation becomes uncontrollable or occurs at inappropriate times, such as laughter at a funeral or news of a friend's misfortune, it becomes a defense against awareness of deeper feelings.

No one wishes to feel pain. We seek what brings pleasure. But reality is not "a chocolate whipped-cream world," as one woman commented. To enjoy adult pleasures, sometimes we first must face youthful hurts. If we go through life laughing at it and telling ourselves, "I don't care what losses I have suffered, I intend to ignore them," we pay a high psychic penalty.

The manic attack was described by Dr. Bertram Lewin as "a flighty dispersed attention to the environment" that fills the person's consciousness and "excludes or crowds into a corner facts and topics that would trouble him or pain him."

One of Freud's favorite jokes showed the connection between the pain of a deep loss—the greatest loss of all—and humor. A prisoner, as he was led to execution on a Monday morning, quipped, "What a way to start the week!" He was trying to deny the fact his life would be lost within minutes.

A feeling of joyousness that is almost manic may follow normal mourning. If mourning is unaccompanied by the guilt inherent in depression, it may end in a heightened sense of well-being, increased sexual potency and a greater capacity for work. Géza Roheim, anthropologist and psychoanalyst, reports that in certain primitive societies mourning after a death is followed by a ceremony of celebration.

Humor is a normal, acceptable way of releasing psychic pain. Humor permits our unpleasurable emotions to rise to the surface but in oblique, controlled fashion. Both jokes and wit turn expected anxiety into a playful feeling. Laughter is the result of relief from the expectation of pain.

But elation, if extreme, denies truth to a dangerous degree in an attempt to override reality. "The notorious holiday from depression: *the manic defence*," Winnicott states (italics his). He adds, "In the manic defence everything serious is negated. Death becomes exaggerated . . . silence becomes noise, there is neither grief nor concern, neither constructive work nor restful pleasure."

The manic masks his deep depression, one that eventually may catch up to him with destructive results. In mania, angry feelings are denied and released in disguised form rather than turned inward as during depression.

One wife noticed that her husband, when in company, turned into a comic, telling joke after joke as the rest of the room roared. But when alone with her, he was morose, uncommunicative.

She asked, "Why can't you be as funny when we're alone as when other people are present?"

He looked at her intently and said, "When I'm with you, I'm myself. I don't have to pretend to be happy."

Through laughter we temporarily overcome many a moment of grief and anger over a loss. We release our feelings in a way that adds no guilt, no depression. For what may be a split second, a repression has been partially lifted.

If we can laugh at what frightens or pains us, we feel less anxious. Anything sacred made to seem profane, anything obscene made to seem innocent, draws our laughter. The targets of much wit and humor are our two most dangerous wishes—our wish to kill and our wish to have unlimited sexual pleasure.

In this permissive society we have learned to laugh at all taboos—even incest. "Incest is best" goes a current gag. The following joke has made the rounds for years:

A Jewish mother talking to a friend says proudly:

"Mine son has just started seeing a shrink."
"What's wrong with him?" asks the friend.
"The shrink says he is sick from something called Oedipus," says the mother.
"Oedipus Schmedipus," says her friend, "as long as he loves his mother."

The man who compulsively tells "dirty" jokes about excretory functions may be combating a loss of sexual potency, regressing to the erotic pleasure of an earlier time. Obscenity may serve as substitute for sexual activity, bringing some gratification, making possible a return to earlier fantasies about sex. Such fantasies are repressed but ready to spring into partial freedom at the tag line of an obscene joke about anality or a sexual perversion.

Dr. Edmund Bergler believed there was both oral and anal gratification when obscene words were spoken. The very mouthing of words like "shit" and "fuck" gives pleasure to the one speaking, as well as the one listening and laughing, he said.

Words may lead to violence but seldom do if they are witty. We hold special affection for jokes that help us laugh our way out of losses. One recent joke makes fun of the "loser":

> *A horse named Pluto, who has lost his last six races, trots*
> *up to the hundred-dollar window at Belmont, plunks down*
> *five hundred dollars and says to the ticket seller, "I want to*
> *bet this on myself. Today I'm going to win."*
>   *The ticket seller's mouth drops open in shock.*
>   *The horse says, "What's the matter? Are you sur-*
> *prised a horse can talk?"*
>   *The seller, recovering, says, "Not at all. I'm stunned*
> *at the idea you think you can win!"*

Jokes may be akin to dreams in that our dreams often contain humor and puns (our unconscious uses puns in a literal sense as part of its language). But the dream serves to guard against pain, while wit brings pleasure. We do not understand the deeper meaning of a dream unless we have been in analysis and have learned to interpret the symbolic message a dream conveys. Dreams reveal our unresolved childhood conflicts, usually kept secret from ourselves because they are painful. Whereas the humor in jokes, even though dealing with the same conflicts, does so in levity and therefore can be accepted at a conscious level.

When we laugh at a loss, as portrayed in a joke, the psychic energy bound up in repressing feelings of grief and anger is discharged in the laughter. The chief source of pleasure in laughter is this release of energy.

We laugh when someone throws a pie in the face of an antagonist. At what are we really laughing? This irreverent reaction is permitted to gratify our childish fantasy of revenge on what we believed the "bad" parent—a David and Goliath story depicted humorously, the pie symbolizing the stone. The weak may laugh at the strong, the fearful at the brave, and the inhibited at the free in the world of humor.

It is difficult to laugh when you feel a deep loss, such as a parent's death, or the loss of a job after twenty years at the same place, or divorce from a mate of thirty years. Too much of your psychic energy must go into fighting off pain.

But the slight state of mania we feel in laughter, according to Dr. Martin Grotjahn, author of *Beyond Laughter*, "is nothing but the state of a bygone time in which we were wont to defray our psychic work with slight expenditure. It is the state of our childhood in which we did not know the comic, were incapable of wit, and did not need humor to make us happy." It was also the state before our repressions set in with a vengeance.

We laugh and, for the moment, forget our losses. That is, if the joke is not on the self. The victim of teasing, or of a practical joke, will feel enraged. He may wish to kill the teaser or the prankster, but usually refrains even from delivering "the killing word," out of fear of inciting violence or, in the case of a practical joke, because he does not want to be thought a poor sport.

To be able to laugh at the self we have to possess a fair share of what psychoanalysts call "ego strength" or self-esteem. It is difficult to laugh at the self because this implies criticism of the self, never a laughing matter. The better we know ourselves, the more likely we are to have a sense of humor about our faults. We realize no one can be perfect and to expect ourselves to be is a remnant of childhood fantasy.

Children feel particularly humiliated and angry when adults laugh at them. A little girl of six, visiting relatives in the country, went upstairs to a bathroom where the toilet looked out on the woods. There was no curtain at the window.

The little girl flew downstairs and said to her mother, "I can't use that bathroom."

"Why not?" asked her mother.

"Because the birds in the trees can look in and see me," she said.

Her mother reassured her, "The birds won't even notice you."

"I don't care if the girl birds do," the little girl said earnestly. "It's the boy birds I mind."

The adults roared, for this released in them early sexual repressions about the anatomical differences between boys and girls. The little girl started to cry, thinking the adults were making fun of her and had to be comforted by her mother.

When does laughter start, both as a sign of pleasure and as defense against a loss? Psychologists who have studied babies observe they smile as early as the eighth day of life. During the first six months, an infant is likely to smile indiscriminately at anyone who coos at him. Then he begins to differentiate between his mother and a stranger. He may welcome both, or only his mother, with a smile.

If a baby loses the ability to smile, or does not smile often, this may be a sign he already suffers from early losses. The inability to smile shows emotional starvation and lack of human contact. It may lead, in extreme cases, to mental retardation (partial death of the mind) or actual physical death.

Laughter and tears are close. As the Bible says, "Even in laughter the heart is sorrowful," recognition that underneath the laughter lie painful fantasies and conflicts.

The clown, whose business it is to make children laugh, sometimes knows well the pain he hides. The late Bert Lahr offstage could turn into a melancholy, shy, superstitious, worried and hypochondriacal man, according to his obituary in *The New York Times*. Lahr once remarked, "I am a sad man. A plumber doesn't go out with his tools. Does a comedian have to be funny on the street?"

Many a comedian who has gone into psychoanalysis discovers the deep sense of loss he has denied with humor, realizing, as Mark Twain said, "The secret source of Humor itself is not joy but sorrow."

Sid Caesar observes that his analysis made him aware "of the eruptions and upheavals of anger and resentment, murderous drives developed in childhood, which had no outlet—the very feelings which could have turned me into a delinquent." He *was* a delinquent in one sense, he adds, in that he took his angry feelings out on the person nearest.

As a result of analysis, he says, "I found I was no longer a child but a grown man, and because I was grown, no problem could loom as large as it had in the days when I was surrounded by giants." He had to face many losses and as he could experience the grief, anger and guilt connected to these losses, his self-esteem grew.

When he was five, his parents quarreled and his mother left their home in Yonkers, New York, to stay with friends in Asbury Park, New Jersey. His father, trying to establish a restaurant, was too busy to look after his small son. He put him on a train with a card around his neck bearing the words "Asbury Park" and asked the conductor to let him off at that stop.

It was raining hard as the train pulled into Asbury Park. The five-year-old boy stepped from the train just in time to see another train pull out in the opposite direction with his mother aboard, her face visible in a window seat. His father had not called his mother to tell her young Sid would be arriving.

Friends who had brought his mother to the station caught sight of him, took him to their home and phoned his parents, now reunited. They asked the friends to keep their son for a few days. He recalls, "If my mother and father had beaten me with baseball bats, they couldn't have hurt me half as much."

To a five-year-old, whose parents have separated, then reunited without him, this kind of loss seems overwhelming—abandonment by both mother and father. It took years before Sid Caesar was able to become aware of the grief and anger he felt as a little boy the day his parents deserted him.

Of such child losses are the lives of comedians, as well as the rest of us, composed. No one escapes the sense of loss he feels as a child when separated from a parent. This is clearly seen by patients in analysis when they separate from the analyst over a holiday or during the long summer vacation. It has become popular to make fun of both the grieving patient and the deserting analyst, proving once again jokes are a way of overcoming the pain of loss.

The comedian who has been on the couch transfers to the analyst all his childhood feelings about his mother and father, his hate as well as his love. During the analysis he deals with conflicting feelings, ones he has denied over the years. He frees himself so he can enjoy bringing people pleasure through laughter. He can now be comic out of a sense of fun, not a sense of pain.

And we who listen to the comedian can laugh out of a sense of fun, not pain, if we are aware of the hidden causes of our laughter. Insight does not kill laughter. It permits a deeper, truer enjoyment of humor.

Though it may seem grim, humor and laughter at the time of the death of a parent may not be as out of place as we think. Most conscious memories are connected to the joy of having known the lost loved one. They are the more acceptable memories, ones that do not have to be repressed.

But part of the process of mourning is to relive *all* the memories about the lost person—both the fond ones and others that may be ludicrous and comic. We should be able to recall scenes of laughter as well as pleasure, part of the work of mourning. And we should not feel guilt for laughing at the lost loved one.

One man, a few days after his father died, felt shocked to find himself laughing at a memory. He recalled the afternoon he saw his father slip on the deck and fall off his boat into the water as everyone on board roared in laughter.

This man's wife asked why he was suddenly laughing. He said apologetically, "I just thought of a funny memory of Dad."

"What was it?" she asked.

He told her, then said, "I didn't mean to put down my father. But it was comical to see this man, who sometimes was an ogre to his children, catapult into the sea."

The son thought he had to be reverential for at least a year after his father's death. But there was no reason for him to feel guilty at enjoying a slight feeling of triumph as he saw the somewhat tyrannical father of childhood get his just desserts. This is why we laugh so heartily at movies when the villain slips on a banana peel.

Laughter eases our losses. Shelley wrote:

> *Our sincerest laughter*
> *With some pain is fraught . . .*

We can use our sense of humor not to forget our devastating losses but to become more honest with ourselves about feelings of grief and rage that underlie the laughter, so we may better complete our mourning.

⑧
Losses
in Growing Up

After we experience the losses of early childhood, as we enter puberty—the age at which it is first possible to beget or bear children—we face different kinds of losses. In most places the legal age of puberty is fixed at fourteen for boys, twelve for girls.

The losses that now occur are connected to our developing sexual and aggressive desires. There is resurgence of the earlier erotic desire for the parent of the opposite sex. In accord with the taboo against incest, repression, which has already set in, is renewed with a vengeance. Girls no longer kiss fathers so ardently, nor boys, their mothers. We remain emotionally tied to parents but our sexual desires now flow to those outside the home.

The love we feel for the parent of the opposite sex is not consciously erotic, nor are we conscious of the hate for our rival, the parent of the same sex. We may hate them but we tell ourselves it is because they are mean or tyrannical. Ideally, a tenderness toward both parents should take over though the earlier sensual desire remains more or less strongly preserved in the unconscious—the whole of the original current continues to exist "underground," as Freud puts it.

As we enter adolescence we are apt to feel a split between our sensual feelings and the new tender feelings. If they never become fused but remain separate, we may feel a romantic, tender love for someone we respect (as we do our mother and father) but do not allow ourselves to think of in sexual terms, and bestow our sensual feelings on someone we do not love romantically or tenderly. This is why men go to prostitutes, for whom they have contempt, or become promiscuous, unable to settle for one woman. Or why women are promiscuous or, in one way or another, pay for sex.

Another kind of loss is involved in adolescent love. Idolatry of the one who is loved usually leads to a loss of identity. When we fall "madly" in love, we are prepared to sacrifice ourselves, if necessary, for the loved one, though reality usually intervenes in time, felling the wild illusions. Also, most of us are not willing to accept for long the loss of identity that is part of such irrational love.

Fantasied losses occur as both boys and girls become acutely aware of the difference in their bodies. Girls are reminded of the lack of the penis they imagined they once had, which they believe taken from them. According to psychoanalysts, every little girl, upon seeing the body of her father or a boy, has the fantasy she has "lost" her penis and all that remains is the remnant clitoris. She is apt to believe her mother "took it away" because she was "bad," as punishment for incestuous fantasies during masturbation.

A boy, on seeing the penisless body of his mother or a girl, fears he may be reduced to that horrendous state if he is "bad" (has incestuous fantasies during masturbation). It is not unusual to see a little boy's hand unconsciously fly to his penis to protect it when scolded by his mother or father. A harsh word, as well as a beating, is unconsciously interpreted by a boy as castrative. Though they have long forgotten it, boys circumcised as babies felt the loss of the foreskin of their penis as they suffered a physical and psychological wound in the interest of cleanliness. This memory may be revived each time they feel threatened by a castrative word or deed.

The adolescent who has not suffered earlier losses too intensely will accept the losses of puberty with ease. He will be able to cope with both his sexual and aggressive desires. Adolescence has been described by parents, teachers and therapists as a time of rebellion. They are apt to dismiss the extreme moods of adolescents as natural at this age. But if an adolescent's behavior is bizarre, if he plunges into moods of intense despair or indulges in acts of violence, he may be hiding grief and anger at losses he cannot handle, that are undermining his self-esteem.

The parents of a fifteen-year-old boy were upset when the teacher called to report their son had been caught stealing the possessions of other children—books, sweaters, food. The teacher said, "We can't understand this. Jimmy has always been a very good boy."

The parents decided to send their son to a therapist to find out why he was suddenly driven to thievery. The therapist learned from Jimmy that his grandfather, a man to whom he had been very close, had recently died. The boy, unable to mourn his loss, had resorted to stealing as a way of trying to compensate for this emotional deprivation.

Bodily and psychological changes occur as the young girl experiences her first menstrual period and the young boy his first moustache or beard. The first menstrual period brings a "loss"—loss of blood, streaming from a sensitive area of her body, one about which she may have strong feelings of disgust. She may also be upset about the loss of blood because it confirms her fantasy she once had a penis but it was cut off (the old wound is bleeding).

The boy with his moustache and beard and the girl with her monthly period both suffer "a loss of innocence." They are no longer entitled to be carefree children. Part of us mourns the need to grow up and take responsibility for ourselves even as we ardently wish for the day we can leave home.

The young girl also is likely to fear "loss of virginity," though today, with girls playing sports at an early age, most do not suffer any pain during the first act of sex. But the first sexual act involves the loss of part of the self, given up in an emotional sense as we share our body with someone else. The young man may feel "engulfed," swallowed up, as he loses his semen. The young woman may feel a loss of the integrity of her body, "invaded" or "penetrated" by a foreign object that might do her harm (make her pregnant). She may also grieve over losing her virtue and feel like a slut, suffering a loss of self-esteem.

If there is a divorce in the family at the time a son or daughter enters adolescence, this represents another kind of loss, one that brings deep grief and anger. The loss of a grandparent, or a physical loss, such as the cutting out of an appendix or pulling of a tooth, is also cause for mourning.

If a parent of an adolescent commits suicide, this makes it very difficult for the adolescent to face his mourning, so devastating his grief and anger. We might also expect that the parent who is so troubled he must kill himself has not been able to provide a secure emotional atmosphere for his children.

One boy of sixteen, whose father committed suicide by taking an overdose of sleeping pills, started to drink heavily and while drunk, assault the girl he was dating. One night, after the girl had him arrested for brutality and he was taken to the police station, his frantic mother decided he had to go into therapy.

The therapist, after talking to the boy, said to the mother, "It's no wonder Charles has been acting so violently. He has been denying his very strong feelings of grief and rage at the father who deserted him in such violent fashion."

"I've been hiding my grief and rage," admitted the mother.

"So Charles has been copying you," said the therapist. "Do you find that strange?"

"No," she said. "I'd better get some help too."

The adolescent unable to mourn his losses finds many ways to deny his feelings. Some study hard, overachieving. Some refuse to study. Others exert themselves in sports or social activities. Still others drink excessively or take to drugs, reaching for addiction as a way of gratifying fantasies rather than face feelings of loss.

Most adolescents, when they reach seventeen or eighteen, leave the physical comfort and emotional security of home (no matter how difficult family life may be, it is familiar and familial and therefore preferable to the unknown). This separation, a large loss in itself, revives memories of earlier losses that are unmourned.

To most adolescents, leaving for college means giving up the family and starting to face the world by the self. Most meet this challenge successfully, having received enough emotional nurturing at home to survive the trauma of such a separation. They surmount the three main problems facing them, described by Dr. Rhoda Lorand, who specializes in the treatment of children and adolescents:

1. Anxiety in relation to the "new" body: difficulties in achieving a firm sense of identity as male or female.

2. Anxiety about greatly increased sexual feelings: the degree and manner of their expression; learning to feel in control, and not at the mercy, of the strong sexual feelings which flood the body, create erotic fantasies and drive toward ever-increasing contact with the opposite sex.

3. Conflicts about remaining safely dependent on the parents, as in the past, versus striking out for independence in all areas: transfer of affection outside the family, establishment of an individual moral code and finding one's life work.

Before he can love someone outside the family, the adolescent must first break childhood attachments to his mother and father. This means, in an emotional sense, that he is able to love them in a more detached way. He is no longer the "little one" idolizing the giant parents whose every word he accepts as "truth." He must now decide whether he differs or agrees with their principles, ethics, ideals and goals. Some parents unfortunately do not fully understand the need for an adolescent to achieve independence. They may rely too heavily on the child's love, perhaps because of unfulfilled needs within themselves.

They feel abandoned as they see their children transfer romantic and sensual love to others.

Some adolescents, when they "fall in love," end up by losing the one they love and feel they will die of a broken heart. But if they can properly mourn this loss they soon recover. Those who are jilted over and over are unconsciously choosing to give love to someone destined to inflict hurt. The broken-heart syndrome is unconsciously invited by the one who needs to suffer because of repressed feelings of anger and guilt over losses of the past.

The number of adolescents who feel so bereft they destroy themselves after the breakup of a love affair, or when they separate from their families, is increasing. In the past decade the suicide rate for college students has more than doubled. On the American campus suicide has become the number two killer, second only to deaths in accidents.

The national rate for suicides of youths between fifteen and nineteen jumped from 2.4 per 100,000 in 1954 to 4 per 100,000 ten years later. There were ten attempts for every successful suicide. Officials of the National Education Association believe there are twice as many child suicides each year as reported on police blotters.

Suicides run 50 percent higher among college students than for the population as a whole. Suicide is nearly half again as frequent among college students as those of the same age not in college, many of whom perhaps have not "lost" their homes but still live in them and work elsewhere.

The need to mourn the loss of a mother and father when a young person leaves for college is evident among students. David Schroedel, psychological counselor at Bennington College, Vermont, mentions the tendency to feel homesick (sick for home) among freshman students who seek help. He comments, "The students tell me they are first aware of the depth of their loss when they go home Thanksgiving and discover their mothers have moved their rooms around. They feel they can't go home again."

The recognition of depression in children and adolescents can be facilitated by the study of their dreams and fantasies, says

Dr. James M. Toolan. The dreams of depressed adolescents often contain dead persons beckoning the adolescent to join them in the other world. Or picture the dreamer as attacked and injured, with loss of either inner or outer parts of the body.

"We interpret the latter to imply a loss of a significant relationship," says Dr. Toolan. Depressed youngsters often relate fantasies of feeling unloved and unwanted, he reports. They find it difficult to identify with members of their family and imagine they belong to another family. Fantasies of running away are common, as are fantasies of being dead, along with the thought that someone (usually their mother and father) will be sorry for having treated them so unkindly.

In addition to loss of family and familiar surroundings, the adolescent in college faces the pressures of getting high grades, being popular, joining the right fraternity or sorority. If there has been too deep an emotional attachment to his parents, the young person setting off for college will feel he is going to his own execution.

Such a youth, if he has an unhappy love affair or fails his studies or cannot make friends, may kill himself as his self-esteem sinks too low for him to bear. The mother of an eighteen-year-old boy who shot himself during his freshman year at college went to a psychoanalyst to overcome her grief. She realized she was a very depressed woman who had unconsciously inflicted her depression on her son as he grew up. He had never attained the emotional strength to separate from her, required when he left for college.

The outside world also presents its threat of losses to youth. The danger of nuclear warfare is ever present, with the lack of peace in many nations. Yet the world has never been a very secure place in which to live. The adolescent in this country during pioneer days, fighting Redcoats and Tories, or living under the terror of Indian raids and massacres, could not have felt very safe. Nor during the Civil War when forced to fight his countrymen.

But the adolescent of today has one advantage over the adolescent of the past. If he feels troubled, he can seek help to understand the feelings of grief and anger connected to his sense of loss. The earlier he receives treatment, the shorter the therapy is likely to be and the more effective. He can then use his great supply of energy wisely, not paralyzing it in alcohol, drugs or other ways of denying hidden feelings.

During adolescence, we start to accept that the magical days of childhood are over. We should be able to study hard, and give thought to the career and the kind of mate we eventually want.

Parents can help by treating their adolescent child with respect, realizing he is well on the way to maturity. Parents can also help by being aware of the losses that occur in adolescence, both those inflicted by reality and those that are part of emotional development.

Parents can also suggest an adolescent get help if he needs it. A growing number of psychoanalysts, psychiatrists, psychologists and social workers specialize in the treatment of adolescents. The first national organization of its kind, the American Society for Adolescent Psychiatry, was recently organized by five hundred psychiatrists from thirty states.

Most colleges have mental health services where psychiatrists and psychologists are available. More students are seeking help than ever before. A study at the University of North Carolina, by Dr. Clifford B. Reifler, Dr. J. Thomas Fox and Dr. Myron B. Liptzin, showed that the number of students seen regularly for emotional disorders during the past ten years increased 10 percent, with women students using the mental health clinics more frequently than men.

One eighteen-year-old student found herself unable to concentrate on her studies. She felt no interest in learning, thought only of how much she missed her home, lived for the weekends she could return to her mother and father.

When she received failing marks at the end of the term, her professor said, "You have a very high I.Q. There is no reason you can't get high marks. Is something troubling you?"

"Nothing specific," she said. "I just can't bring myself to study." She added in apology, "I'm too homesick."

The professor persuaded her to go to the mental health clinic on the campus. She talked to a psychiatrist and slowly became aware she had been mourning separation from her mother. As she was able to express her grief and her anger, she found energy returning for her studies. By the end of the second term her marks were among the highest in the class.

Separation from a mother and father can be felt either as a step toward independence or an abandonment. The degree to which an adolescent has accepted past losses determines whether he is able to look upon his entrance into the world of reality as another devastating loss that brings only pain or a liberation that brings pleasure.

9
Losses of Later Life

When we fall in love and marry, in a very deep sense we lose our mother and father, brothers and sisters. "Forsaking all others" orders the marriage vow. Unless these words are accepted emotionally as well as intellectually by both husband and wife, trouble lies ahead. Loyalties will be divided and jealousy and anger apt to erupt.

The traditional mother versus daughter-in-law controversy is based on a failure to give up familial allegiances. Sometimes a mother refuses to relinquish emotional possession of a son or daughter, so the marriage does not stand a chance. Sometimes a bride or groom wants the mate to break complete ties with parents, demanding full emotional possession, also an unreasonable request.

If the newly married person has been able to merge tender and sensual feelings, he will move more away from his parents toward his new love. Otherwise he will not be able to give or to share the depth of love necessary for a successful marriage. Sensual feelings alone do not lead to lasting love.

When we marry, it is natural to feel the loss of part of the self. We now have to share privacy and time—share meals, bed, bathroom, friends, leisure hours, vacations. We will feel some sorrow and anger at these losses but if we are aware of our feelings we can then accept the loss of part of ourselves as well worth the many new rewards of intimacy with a loved one. Some are not able to accept the loss of privacy and complete independence and never feel at ease in marriage.

The person who, though married and ostensibly willing to share all decisions, must dominate, has not accepted the loss of part of himself. His infantile need to be "the boss" may eventually destroy the marriage if his mate decides to rebel.

A loss of part of the self is felt again, by both men and women, when a baby is born. In a practical sense, they have lost the intimacy they shared. There is now a third person, and a demanding one, who has emphatically entered their lives.

The husband may feel he has lost part of his wife's love as he watches the deep attachment that develops between mother and baby. A man whose self-esteem is high knows his baby needs a mother's love and measures this against his feelings of temporary loss. But the husband who still feels angry because of un-mourned childhood losses may be unduly jealous of the baby, resenting it much of the time.

At the birth of the baby the mother may feel loss of the fetus, which she has been nourishing within, and this awakens memories of earlier losses. If a woman has never come to terms with the earlier losses, she may treat her child as though it were sent to make up for past losses, adding to the difficulties the child faces in separating from her.

Abortions, whether in or out of marriage, always create a

sense of loss, even in those women who insist they do not want the child. Whatever rational reason a woman gives for aborting her baby, in her unconscious she will feel a deep sense of loss, perhaps even imagine she is a murderer. She will feel emotional pain at the injury inflicted as the baby is cut out of her unnaturally.

This is not to oppose abortion, the only humane approach to solving the conflicts of many pregnant women, but to point out the woman will suffer a deep sense of loss after the abortion. She has to weigh this loss against what, to her, may be the far greater loss in self-esteem if she gave birth to an unwanted child.

One woman of twenty-eight, unmarried, told her psychoanalyst, "I had two abortions. Both fathers were married men. To me, the stigma of bringing up a baby without a father was more terrifying than bearing two illegitimate children. I would have hated them."

The woman who, for whatever reason, has not borne a child will also suffer a deep sense of loss, even if she insists she never wanted children. If she is able to face her deeper feelings, she realizes she has missed one of life's most satisfying experiences, nurturing and raising a child. The capacity for mother love exists in every woman and, if unfulfilled, the woman is bound to feel a deep loss.

As we enter middle age, new losses face us. For an increasing number of men and women, divorce becomes part of reality. Divorce is always felt as a loss, even when both husband and wife seek it. It is difficult to spend years with someone without feeling sorrow and anger when they leave or you walk away. If only because the loss reawakens the pain of past losses.

In the years between forty and sixty our bodies start to age. The first wrinkle on our face produces the feeling of a loss—"the lost life," "the lost opportunities," "the lost joys." The aging of her body makes a woman feel a loss of sexuality, and a man, loss of potency. These losses may drive men and women into affairs as they try to restore self-esteem. But then guilt follows, leaving only depressed feelings, nothing solved.

Middle age means menopause for women, both an emotional and a physical loss. Women "lose" the flow of monthly blood, which means the loss of ability to bear babies. In a sense, they now feel useless, no longer needed for the survival of the species.

Though many women feel sexless after menopause, which may occur between forty-five and fifty-three (the average age is forty-seven, according to authorities), investigators in sexual behavior report sexual desire persists in a heightened degree for many years after menopause if the woman overcomes her feelings of loss.

While men also become depressed at the thought of growing old, a man is apt to feel more secure because usually he can keep on achieving in business or professional activities (this is true, too, for the business, professional or creative woman). Some men even discover themselves creatively at this time, following in the footsteps of Sherwood Anderson and Paul Gauguin, who, during middle age, decided they did not like what they were doing, carved out new careers and became artistic successes.

But all too often middle-aged men and women, believing their lives slipping away, ask such tormenting questions as: "Is this all there is to life?" "What have I achieved?" "Why do I feel so empty and hopeless?" Middle age has been called "the critical age."

But it need not be if losses can be faced, if the feelings that accompany a loss are allowed into awareness. If a life has held love, friendships, pursuit of a rewarding career or avocation, middle age should hold no special fears.

It can be a time of further growth. With children out of the house, there is new leisure for exploration of interests, new understanding of the self and others. Dr. Alberta B. Szalita, psychoanalyst, says of the middle-aged:

> *Struggle, regret and despair are active emotions of the process of mourning and grief; active psychodynamic forces lead, in the final analysis, to a solution, to a new distribution of energy and interests, and to acceptable and often enjoyable senescence. But if hopelessness and helplessness prevail, the outcome is fearful surrender.*

During middle age we are apt to lose a part of our body—a tooth, a gallbladder, an appendix, and women, perhaps a breast or uterus. After each surgery, no matter how minor, deep psychological loss is felt. When a surgeon's knife cuts into the body there is not only loss of blood but also loss of the sanctity of flesh, as well as loss of an organ. The body responds quickly in the healing of the wound but the psyche does not heal as quickly.

Surgery inflicts not only the pain of the operation but reminder of the pain of past psychic losses, such as the death of someone loved or feelings of castration. Men may feel sexually impotent after an operation and women, unattractive sexually. Again, it is a question of being aware of the despair and rage at a loss even though the loss is suffered so our life may be saved. The unconscious accepts no rational reasons. It knows there is only pain rather than the pleasure it seeks.

A woman of fifty, who was divorced, had to undergo a mastectomy and at first thought she could not survive psychologically. She was in analysis and managed, with the analyst's help, to face her feelings of grief and rage. A few months after the operation she told him, "I no longer feel suicidal. I realize my feelings at losing a breast, while partially realistic, were so intense because they related to my fantasy as a girl that I had lost a precious part of my body."

Within six months she met a man who, sure of his manliness, was not terrified because she was minus a breast and loved her for her personal qualities of warmth, understanding and generosity.

After an operation we have the wish to restore what is lost, which explains why so many ex-patients overeat. The loss in an operation differs from the loss of a loved one in that detachment from another is easier than detachment from the self. We can admit anger and disparagement of another and thus loosen our attachment until finally we give him up. But when part of ourselves is lost, it is difficult to become angry and disparage the self.

One woman, after a gallbladder operation. regained the thirty pounds she had lost during the year her diet was restricted to bland foods. She became very angry at herself. She was in analysis and asked the analyst, "Why can't I control my eating?"

"You are eating to make up for the lost gallbladder," he said.

"I was glad to get rid of it!" she protested.

"That has nothing to do with mourning a lost part of the self," said the analyst.

He also pointed out the loss of the gallbladder reawakened memories of past losses and she was eating to make up for them, too.

Why did a number of executives hurl themselves out of high-floor windows when they lost heavily in the stock market crash of 1929? They felt castrated—the loss of money stirred earlier fears of loss of manhood and loss of feces, which is originally imagined as part of the self that becomes detached and lost.

In middle age one of the deepest losses may be the death of a parent. The excruciating impact of a parent's death is due to a feeling of complete and final severance from someone loved since birth. It is no doubt life's most painful emotional experience as it stirs memories of all past separations and losses.

Today, because of modern medical advances, many old people live on though extremely incapacitated and sons and daughters find themselves troubled by conflicting feelings. A well-known interior decorator has a mother confined to her home with a nurse. The daughter says she feels grief, guilt and shame, and the fear the same fate will befall her. "I see my mother turn into an infant before my eyes—an infant for whom there's no hope for growth," she says. A parent's regression to infancy is difficult for most of us to bear. We cannot tolerate the infant in ourselves, much less seeing a parent, who has been like a god to us, become incontinent, dependent, in need of total care.

As Lillian Hellman comments in her book *Pentimento*, "It is not good to see people who have been pretending strength all their lives lose it even for a minute.''

There is a difference between the trauma of the sudden, unexpected death of a parent and the knowledge in advance a parent is ill and will eventually die. If a parent is confined to a nursing home for years, the son or daughter is able to gradually mourn the approaching loss. This eases the shock of death when it occurs, though even then the mourning process must be experienced.

Christmas also reminds us of lost parents and of lost gifts—gifts represent love in the unconscious. We expect a certain sadness at holidays, especially Christmas as we recall our lost childhood, of which Christmas was probably the most joyous day.

Other anniversary mourning may be connected to birthdays of loved ones, a holiday that holds special memories such as New Year's Eve or the Fourth of July, or the anniversary of a childhood trauma, such as the death of a beloved grandmother. ''The parent-child identifications present at the anniversary time are the 'traumatized' child of old as well as the parent of old, who is expected to die,'' says Dr. George Pollock.

Some sons and daughters fear they will die at the age their parent died. Psychoanalysts point out one of the reasons for this fear, a sign of unfulfilled mourning, is the repressed anger the son or daughter felt as a child for the parent. When the parent dies, the child unconsciously believes he has caused the death and in accordance with the law of the talion—an eye for an eye—that rules the unconscious, feels he deserves to die at the same age as his parent as punishment.

Old age brings its special losses, including retirement—loss of job or career unless one continues creative work at home. Recent pressures in Congress may change the age of retirement from sixty-five to seventy in recognition of the many losses vigorous people suffer emotionally when forced to give up work of which they are still capable.

Retirement, when it is not welcome, brings a loss of dignity, of self-esteem and faith in the ability to produce. Many men and women are willing and able to work until the day they die. The loss felt when forced to retire has undoubtedly brought early deaths to some, so deep their suppressed despair and fury. We should be able to choose whether we wish to retire or keep working if our ability to produce has not diminished.

The older we become, the more losses we face in reality as relatives and friends die: "The older one gets, the more one experiences the loss of significant persons. The aging person has, of necessity, to undergo more and more grief reactions."

These are the words of Dr. Martin A. Berezin, who has studied the emotional processes of aging. He points out the aged suffer losses not encountered earlier in life. These losses fall into three groups: job, status and money; bodily functions and abilities; independence and self-respect. Such losses are "invariably encountered in varying degree by all aged people," he maintains.

A woman of seventy-four came to Berezin's office recently and said, "I would like to be psychoanalyzed."

He looked at her thoughtfully, as though to ask why anyone over seventy would start psychoanalysis.

She said, in explanation to his unasked question, "Doctor, all I have left is my future."

This woman had not given up life as lost just because she was in her seventies. She felt she wanted to know more about her deeper feelings so she would get the most out of her later years.

She was not defeated by the loss of what Dr. Pollock calls "the self that is not to be," a loss pessimistically accepted by many older persons.

No generalities can be made about "the aged," just as no generalities can be made about any group. Each individual must be considered in terms of his unique experiences. Dr. Grotjahn, who has studied the psychological processes of aging and engaged in psychoanalytic treatment of the aged, describes three different ways individuals may react to the problems of aging.

The first is the normal, natural way, which aims at the acceptance "of a life as it has been lived" and the integration of old age with the whole life.

The second is with increased rigidity and fear, as the ego

"tries to hold the line of defenses according to the pattern of previous more or less neurotic adjustment."

The third reaction may be, in cases where the losses are felt as devastating, with psychosis or a depression that ends in suicide.

Growing old, particularly in this nation where so much emphasis is placed on keeping young and beautiful, may be felt as a deep wound to self-esteem. Further denigration of the image of the self may occur as the face takes on wrinkles, the hair turns gray, then white, and eating becomes the only pleasure and solace, adding unsightly pounds. The self is felt as sexless, unwanted, ugly.

Grotjahn believes the emotional disturbances of old age are often a defense against castration anxiety. While, in the unconscious, there is no awareness of our own death, he says: "Our unconscious knows all about the death, mutilation and murder of others. Our unconscious also knows the dangers of mutilation and castration which we anticipate with fear and anxiety. In the psychotherapy of elderly people, these castration anxieties have to be analyzed before death anxiety can be dealt with."

He continues: "Overwhelming fear of death in the elderly hides castration anxiety and may lead to the desire to die. It is extremely important in the practice of psychotherapy with the elderly to realize that a good part of death anxiety is a symbolic representation of castration anxiety activated by the narcissistic trauma of aging."

Aging thus may deal a severe blow to our self-esteem. But if that self-esteem has been high throughout life, we not only accept the losses of aging but find rewards in a time of life free from the reality pressures of the past—to get married, to raise children, to earn a living. There is time to enjoy the quiet pleasures of life, perhaps to be creative in new ways.

After all, Sir Winston Churchill was sixty-five on the eve of leading his nation through World War II, Benjamin Franklin was seventy when he signed the Declaration of Independence and Michelangelo was eighty-eight when he sculpted his final *Pietà*.

10
How to Face Losses

Let us put together what the pioneer researchers on mourning found to help us understand and ease the tormenting feelings of loss we so often experience.

Freud discovered there was a difference between the natural mourning that takes place following the death of a loved one and "melancholia" or a lasting depression. The difference: the bereaved person who could go through the natural mourning process felt no guilt. The guilt of the depressed person came from his repressed feelings of anger at the lost loved one.

Other psychoanalysts then studied in depth the emotions we all experience after a loss, principally grief, despair and rage. These emotions represent the natural reactions of body and mind to a loss. They are as automatic as if someone attacked us physically and we prepared, in Cannon's words, for "fight or flight." A verbal insult, a danger to self-esteem, is just as much an attack on our person as a gun fired at our heart.

But it is difficult to accept that a psychic hurt can be as devastating as a physical one. Perhaps because the wound is not evident. No blood pours forth. No visible scars appear. But within us occurs "internal bleeding" and searing scars, though intangible.

Just as our body heals naturally after a physical wound, so the mind attempts to heal naturally after the emotional wound inflicted by a loss. Unfortunately, many of us inhibit the natural process of healing that follows a loss, because we have been taught *not* to express or to allow ourselves to feel our deeper emotions.

We go through life carrying a burden of repressed emotions that demand an undue amount of our psychic and physical energy. We inflict extra anguish on ourselves as we bypass the natural process of mourning.

After a loss we should experience emotionally our protest against the loss, including trying to recover what is lost. Then we should feel fury and desire for revenge on whoever caused the loss. Then our grief. If we are able to be aware of all these emotions, there will follow a sense of detachment from the person or thing or ideal lost, out of which flows acceptance of the loss.

We never "get rid of" the feeling of loss, for we never "get rid of" any feeling. The memory of an emotion and the experience that caused it remains always in the unconscious part of our mind where memories are stored. But with acceptance of a loss, we are able to *suppress* feelings, a conscious choice, rather than *repress* feelings, an unconscious, automatic act caused by the wish to deny what we feel.

To accept a loss means we have faced our deepest feelings about that loss. We have not taken flight from what we believe dangerous emotions. They will pursue us anyhow since they are the enemies within, relentlessly demanding to be confronted.

The mourning process is the same whether the loss is a deep one, such as the death of a mother or father, or a minor one, such as the loss of self-esteem felt when someone we love criticizes us.

It merely takes a longer time for the deeper loss to be accepted.

Compare the way we feel after we have lost, say a ten-dollar bet at the racetrack, and at the death of a friend. The reactions are the same—shock, dismay, sorrow, the wish to recover what is lost, anger, then acceptance. We are over the loss of the ten-dollar bet in two minutes, in time to study the horses for the next race as we try to make restitution. But it may take a year to fully mourn the loss of a friend.

We live in a fantasy world if we believe we can go through life without losses. Or without mourning our losses, both the large losses and the smaller losses of everyday living. We cannot escape the normal miseries of life which include a certain amount of loss.

How can we effectively handle our losses—the large and the small? Both those dealt by the outside world and those inflicted by our inner world of psychic reality.

There is only one way. *By knowing what we feel.* By refusing to deny feelings of sorrow and of fury. To deny or inhibit a feeling is not to control but to repress. True control comes in being able to face a feeling even though it may be painful for the moment.

As Dr. Lawrence Friedman told me recently, "In this age of the neutron bomb and genetic manipulation, human emotions have a difficult time. If we manage to survive, it will not be by cloning or the monstrosities we create with our intellect, but by the efforts of people who are capable of feeling—of loving, hating, having pleasure and suffering."

We suffer when a loss occurs and we should not try to avoid the shock, the hurt, the sadness and the rage. We should try to accept every emotion we feel as natural reaction to a threat to our psychological survival.

We may judiciously choose to flee an adversary but we should always choose to face a feeling. If we flee feelings of grief and anger, we will always feel helpless and hopeless in the face of a loss. Only by becoming aware of the emotions involved in a sense of loss and experiencing these emotions as fully as possible can we keep ourselves from being overwhelmed or terrorized by

*the loss. Our bodies and minds possess the capacity to feel sor-
row and rage so we* can *eventually accept a devastating grief.*

If we become aware of what we feel when we suffer a loss, we make sure the loss will not have a destructive effect on the rest of our life. If we can mourn past losses, we will not overreact to current losses that do not warrant intense grief or anger. We can differentiate between losses that are part of reality and losses that stem from fantasy.

Our overreactions to the losses of everyday life that cause a drop in self-esteem, such as the sarcastic insults, the broken appointments, the snubbings, are minuscule reproduction of the devastating feelings we have repressed over the years connected to earlier losses. We have not properly mourned these first losses which still haunt us, sparked to memory by a current loss.

One woman lost her purse which contained twenty dollars, a BankAmericard, a tortoiseshell comb and cosmetics. These were all easily replaceable items, yet she felt inconsolable, bursting into tears when she reached home.

When she told her analyst how she had behaved, he asked, "Why were you so upset by the loss of a few *things*?"

"I felt I had lost part of myself," she said.

"You could live very well without any of the objects you lost," he said. "There was nothing essential or irreplaceable."

"I am *always* losing things and hating myself for it," she wailed.

"It isn't the things—it's what they stand for," he said.

She was silent a moment, then said, "Like people, you mean?"

"Whom are you thinking of?"

"My father left home when I was nine to marry another woman. My mother remarried the next year and sent me to board-ing school."

She started to cry and to rage at her parents for the losses they had caused her. She had felt utterly rejected, never able to admit her feelings about the earlier, very threatening losses of her life.

It seems a sad fact that many of us go through life contain-ing within ourselves an unfulfilled need to mourn earlier losses.

As children we were not encouraged to feel the natural sorrow and rage that followed the ordinary losses that befell us in growing up. Instead, our parents conveyed the feeling it was shameful and embarrassing to express any emotion over a loss. This created within us a conflict between two opposing wishes—the wish to cry and rage, our natural impulses, and the wish not to cry or rage so our mother and father would continue to love us.

It is natural, nay *essential*, for us to mourn both the small and the large losses that occur during our lives. The large losses, such as the death of loved ones, are often easier to accept—at least the grief part of the mourning. It is taken for granted we feel sorrow when someone we love dies. We carry on the tradition of the deceased leaving his possessions to his loved ones, as though if we own some object belonging to the dead person—a ring, an article of clothing, or money—we are reassured he is not completely lost. We invest the object with a magical quality as if by possessing it we still keep part of the lost loved one with us.

Acceptance of the death of a parent, however, may take a long time if feelings are denied. A woman who lost a father told her analyst, "I can accept his loss only as I remember specific times in my life when I loved him and when I hated him, and feel both my sorrow and my anger when he tried to control me."

It helps to try to relate a current loss to a past one and live through feelings repressed at the time of the past loss. We read an obituary of someone we barely knew yet feel like crying at this comparative stranger's death. If we let ourselves think about the deaths of those close to us, whom we loved/hated, then feel our grief and anger, we will be doing the work of mourning. We have to recall memories of the moments we hated the lost one as well as the times we loved him dearly.

One woman whose mother had been dead four years was unable to detach herself emotionally. At an analytic session she said, "I feel so. guilty when I think of Mother."

"Why?" asked the analyst.

She was silent, then said, "This isn't easy to speak about. But I realize I must tell you everything I think. Mother left me a lot of money, as you know. Well, those three years she spent in a nursing home, I would say to myself, 'Why doesn't she die right now so I can have her money, which is no good to her, and live more comfortably?' And I feel such guilt at wishing her dead."

"This wish is natural in a child when a parent has money," said the analyst. "You were conscious of such a wish. I think your guilt has to do with other wishes. Wishes you are hiding from yourself."

"Such as?"

"The earlier wish as a little girl that your mother would die. Disappear forever. So you and your adored father could live alone, two against the world."

The woman started to cry. "I know you're right," she said through tears, "but it's so hard to accept."

It is difficult to admit forbidden wishes and face the conflicts they aroused when we were children. It is these unresolved conflicts, however, that keep us from being fully able to mourn a loss.

But it is not primarily for the dead most of us mourn during the course of our lives. We mourn mostly what we think of as "the little losses." We walk around feeling a vague sense of despair at being deprived of something we cannot replace. We say, "I feel lost." Or, "I feel blue" (babies turn blue when they suffer a loss of air).

An old English ballad, "The Friar of Orders Gray," by Thomas Percy, goes:

> *Since grief but aggravates thy loss,*
> *Grieve not for what is past.*

This is what most of us have been brought up to believe. But just the reverse is true. We *have* to grieve after a loss if we are to accept it. Too many of us exist emotionally stifled because we feel it is "wrong" to confess feelings of hurt and sadness, anger and desire for revenge.

"Who breathes must suffer, and who thinks must mourn," said the poet Matthew Prior. If we can mourn at the time of a loss, it will save weeks, months, perhaps years of unfulfilled mourning and self-destructive behavior. Completing the mourning process allows us to put aside the sorrow of both the present and the past. We can then give full emotional energy to the joyous, productive, creative part of life.

Grief and rage are the two emotions we are likely to repress at a loss. Let us first consider our sorrow and despair.

As Shakespeare's King Henry VI says: "To weep is to make less the depth of grief." But most of us possess dammed-up tears from childhood as well as the adult tears we dare not permit flow. Men particularly, in our culture, are deprived of this crucial outlet in facing a loss since it is considered unmanly to shed a tear, much less sob.

Unfortunately our wish to cry is thwarted in its natural expression almost from birth, except for that moment immediately after we enter the world when we emit our first cry. The doctor will smack us to produce the cry if we do not utter it, for it can be delayed only at the risk of our life. If a baby cannot breathe, he will die. Thus our first breath of life is associated with crying and the first great alarm shown by others is over whether we will cry—live or die.

A baby cries for food when he is hungry or when he feels pain or discomfort. Crying is fixed very early in our mind as a natural way of relieving distress. But many parents become angered or irritated at an infant's wailing so the infant learns to inhibit his cries. One of the first commands many of us hear in life is "Stop that crying!" Every so often a story appears in the newspapers about a father or mother who has beaten or killed a baby because it would not stop crying.

The taboo against tears continues as we grow up. Crying brings contempt from the outer world. A boy who dares show a tear when hurt by a baseball or in a football tackle is thought a sissy. A girl is permitted to cry once in a while but most girls refuse to cry even if they are hurt physically or emotionally, not wishing to be thought the "weaker sex." Society regards as inferior anyone who sheds tears when he feels hurt, angry or lonely. The medals belong to the stoics, pained though they may feel within.

There is, fortunately, at least one place men, women and children are encouraged to allow tears to flow and to express the grief they feel over losses—in the psychotherapist's office. There

they become familiar with feelings buried under denials and pre-
tenses.

A man attending a dinner party was called to the phone. He
returned to the table and explained, "My best friend was just
killed in a plane crash." The other guests expressed polite, re-
strained sympathy. He sat down to resume eating but his grief
was so overwhelming he burst into tears. Everyone was embar-
rassed to see a grown man cry except one guest, a lawyer, who
was in analysis and had shed tears on the couch.

He walked over to the grieving man, put an arm around his
shoulders and said, "Cry it out. You obviously have lost someone dear."

Tears are so forbidden it is possible their repression may be
the chief cause of the common cold, whose origin has puzzled
man for centuries. The close connection between catching a cold
and holding back tears was described in my book *Your Mind Can
Stop the Common Cold*.

I was led to this conclusion in part by Dr. Franz Alexander's
explanation of how an ulcer forms. The empty stomach of the
ulcer patient constantly reacts as though preparing to receive
food, as if responding to the wish to be excessively fed. Could
not another physical reaction of the body, as it responded to the
wish to cry, explain the common cold? What about comparing the
reaction of the nose of the person who catches a cold with the
stomach of the ulcer patient acting as though it expected food?
What is the nose expecting?

Tears. Tears, unshed, are awaited by the nose as the turbinates swell, just as they do when real tears are expected. The nose
physically responds to a wish to weep but a wish we repress, a
wish diverted from direct delivery to the tear ducts by a conscious
censor of the mind that instructs, "Don't cry!"

But the nose, directed by another level of thought from our
unconscious, which controls the automatic physiological processes of the body, responds as it would naturally to a hurt, ignoring
the order not to cry. The turbinates become engorged and *stay*
engorged, awaiting tears that never flow. Just as the stomach of
the ulcer patient awaits food that is wished for but not as yet
eaten and forms an ulcer because of its hyperactivity.

The prolonged engorgement of the turbinates in the nose weakens its resistance to viruses always in the air or residing in the nose in moderate number. The weakened condition is due to the fact that the swelling of the turbinates blocks the open passages of the nose, preventing the air from sweeping infectious viruses through the nose and into the stomach where they are destroyed. Instead, the viruses cluster in the nose and multiply, causing the infection we know as the common cold.

It should not be surprising that when we suffer a loss, which causes sorrow, this is reflected in the activity of our nose, which we have to blow when it becomes clogged with tears. The nose is also closely involved with the two things we must take into our body to keep alive—air through breathing, and food, through smelling (primitive man could tell whether food was decayed or poisonous by sniffing it, even as we must sometimes do today).

Our tears are protective in two ways. They flow to defend against a foreign body in the eye, such as an irritating or damaging piece of dust or dirt, strong gas, a very powerful light or a cold wind. And they *defend against feelings of grief, sorrow and hurt*.

Thus, the nose is the physical outlet for the emotions of grief and sorrow that ordinarily require the blowing of the nose. And even though we shed no tears during the common cold, we blow our nose many times over as though tears were flowing. Because the wish to cry has been repressed, the real tears are bypassed. But there has been symbolic replacement.

When we mourn a loss, our tears have a healing power. But if we repress our wish to cry, we may catch cold or infect our body in other ways. Unfortunately, we are brought up to believe the holding back of tears will enhance our self-esteem. Thus to catch a cold becomes part of the approved survival system as, in disguised fashion, the nose cries through the drippings that simulate tears and the blowings that are part of getting rid of tears. And as usually happens when we repress awareness of a feeling, we inflict punishment on ourselves—days of work lost, sleepless nights, lowered self-esteem.

A psychoanalyst described the common cold as "the unconscious weeps." Commenting on this, Dr. Walter A. Stewart says, "The unconscious never weeps—the ego weeps. The unconscious knows no remorse, only the conscious sorrows."

Of the common cold, he states: "It is ubiquitous and represents so many hidden wishes, no wonder it is difficult to find a vaccine to prevent it. But in a general sense, you might say the common cold represents the wish to cry, thwarted in its natural expression and forced to seek an outlet in an appropriate, or sympathetic channel of the body."

The common cold occurs so frequently among so many of us, especially children, it would appear proof of a vast universal need to shed tears held back after a loss, out of the mistaken belief that to cry is shameful, a sign of weakness.

Our natural reaction to a loss is tears but if, for some reason, we inhibit the tears when we feel sorrow, denying physical outlet to our wish to cry, the chemical balance of our body is disturbed. The body then automatically seeks to restore the balance. The organ affected by the emotion, in this case the nose, *acts as though* the natural reaction to a wish to cry were taking place as the body seeks to restore equilibrium.

When we repress a wish, we may avoid facing humiliating and shameful feelings but we inflict pain on our body. Pain is one way the body speaks to us in symbolic language, telling of repressed wishes. There is no organ of the body that cannot be used in the interest of repressed sexual and aggressive feelings, providing what psychoanalysts call partial gratification.

The specific connection between a repressed wish to cry and the common cold has been noted by psychoanalysts. They report that patients prone to catch colds, once they shed tears on the couch, discover their colds disappear.

Dr. Bruce Ruddick studied twenty patients who were suffering from the common cold. He concluded the cold "could be a grief reaction to a separation or loss, either real or threatened, present or past, or to the anniversary of a loss."

The common cold also, in his words, represented an unconscious attempt "to regain the lost object through respiratory introjection." This psychic process involves the fantasy of breathing in, like air, the image of the lost loved one. Psychoanalysts say this is the first way an infant tries to possess his mother in that he knows how to breathe even before he learns to eat—the use of the mouth for introjection is called oral incorporation.

Ruddick also found many patients unconsciously mourned a loss on the anniversary of that loss, by catching a cold. One man of twenty-six, suffering a severe cold, told Ruddick he had caught it the previous afternoon. He then described his dream that night: "My mother was in your office crying and making an awful fuss."

Ruddick asked, "Do you think she was mourning something?"

"Maybe she was," the man said. "Her father died about a year ago."

"Do you remember the day?"

The man thought for a moment, then said in astonishment, "Why, it was yesterday! January fourteenth."

"The day you caught the cold," said Ruddick.

This man had been very close to his grandfather and, mourning his death, unconsciously was trying to restore his grandfather through respiratory introjection via the cold.

Another patient caught cold ten years to the day his father died. Still another, two years after his analysis ended, observed a different kind of anniversary loss. He caught a cold, then dreamed he was furious at his ex-analyst for not adequately preparing him for the end of the analysis. The appearance of the cold, coinciding with the reappearance of the analyst in the dream, made him aware he had caught the cold exactly two years to the day he had ended analysis. His dream revealed repressed feelings of anger and despair, part of mourning.

An actress had a sinus condition so severe it kept her from performing. She went to a psychoanalyst on advice of her doctor, who could find no physical cause. The first day on the couch she burst into tears and, as she left the analyst's office discovered her sinuses were clear. During ensuing sessions she cried much of the hour and within a few weeks found the sinus condition had completely vanished. She remained in analysis, realizing her illness had masked deep feelings of sorrow and rage.

Another woman, who caught colds all winter, went into analysis when her marriage broke up. She slowly became aware, through the shedding of tears, she had spent most of her life denying feelings of grief. She told the analyst, "I've choked back all my real feelings."

At the end of her analysis she realized she had not caught a cold in a year. She said to the analyst, "My colds were a giveaway to the torment underneath."

Dr. George Groddeck, a physician in Germany, who studied the relationship between physical and emotional illness, asserted: "One thing remains to be said: disease gives evidence of deceit, or a lie. The way of sickness is no honourable way, and whoever thinks it possible and desirable to be honest would do well to teach the It [the Id, the unconscious] other ways of action."

He also declared perceptively: "Our brains are being overtaxed not by earnest seeking after truth, but by the continual effort to suppress our real nature—primitive, purposeful, double-sexed and double-imaged—in favour of what we take to be the real, the objective. The attempt to deny our nature is bound to fail, and results only in excessive repression; this again turns what is natural and healthy into poison."

It is difficult for an adult to admit he wants to cry because someone has hurled a cruel word or he is rejected by a group he wants to join. Most of us would rather be thought a cheat, a coward, a thief, perhaps even a murderer, than confess to ourselves, let alone others, we feel childish enough to cry.

So instead of shedding tears or uttering sobs for the lost, comforting mother of childhood who, at the moment, we wished were near to make the world right, we deny such shameful feelings and catch a cold instead.

A man asked to resign from his job as an account executive came down with a cold for the first time in years. He was in analysis and, on the couch, announced grimly, "I've been fired. They claim I'm incompetent."

"How do you feel?" asked the analyst.

"Damned glad!" he said. "I couldn't have stood that office another day."

"You've talked for months about how you hated it."

The man burst out, "But *I* wanted to be the one to decide

when to quit. I didn't want to be thrown out, like an old dirty sock."

"I would think you'd feel very angry," said the analyst.

"I'm mad as hell!" There was explosive fury in the man's voice. "I wanted to tell Bob [his employer] what I thought of him, but didn't dare."

"The important thing is *you* know how angry you are," said the analyst. "You don't have to act on it—just know it."

The man suddenly found tears in his eyes. He started to cry. He took out his handkerchief, blew his nose several times.

"Excuse me," he said. "I didn't mean to act like a baby."

"What's wrong with tears?" said the analyst. "Adults can feel just as hurt as a child. When you want to cry, cry. Don't hold back."

As the man rose from the couch at the end of the session, he said in surprise, "My nose isn't stuffed. My cold seems gone."

He had been able to express grief and anger after a demeaning experience. He later told the analyst he realized he had been asking to be fired because he disliked both his employer and the work. He was able soon after to find a job managing a firm of architects, which he far preferred.

The repressed anger in someone who has caught a cold is obvious to those who are close. One husband wrote his wife a couplet:

> *Darling I have got a cold*
> *Why do you your love withhold?*

She answered:

> *Darling I must the hour await*
> *Until the hate in your cold abate.*

A woman consulted Dr. Leon Saul because, she said, she was unable to have a sexual relationship with a man even though she felt an intense longing for love. She seemed frightened, inhibited about any expression of sexual desire, Dr. Saul noted.

She suffered from an almost constant outbreak of hives on

her face, particularly around her eyes, and sometimes a swelling of the throat. Medical tests showed she was not allergic to any specific food or anything in the air such as pollen. She also had migraine headaches and often woke in terror from nightmares.

Her mother had divorced a previous husband to marry the patient's father when both were not yet twenty. When the patient, the oldest child, was one and a half, a sister was born. Half a year later the mother died, it was rumored, after her husband assaulted her. He then married a divorcée with three children, placing his two daughters in an orphanage. The patient was four at the time.

After a year, the father took his two daughters back into his home. He was an irresponsible man not only toward his daughters but in general. He took part in illicit business deals, serving several short terms in prison. His second wife did not like the patient and often falsely accused her of misbehavior, whereupon her father beat her. Her childhood was much like Cinderella's, a life of drudgery and abuse, according to Dr. Saul. She had no pleasure or escape from pain except in daydreams.

During her analysis the patient showed an intense longing for the mother she had known only the first two years of her life and who, she felt, had deserted her by dying. Whenever this longing became intense, she would break out in hives.

She often dreamed of reaching for someone or something that kept slipping from her grasp. One day as she described such a dream to Dr. Saul, she started to cry. There was no outbreak of hives that day. As she could cry on the couch, she no longer needed the hives.

Most of us, like this woman, bravely hold back tears no matter what hardships and cruelties we have suffered. Yet we would suffer far less, emotionally and physically, if we would cry when we felt like it. It is well known we feel better after "a good cry." We have to face the child in ourselves at times, especially the hurt child.

Many parents believe they can do or say anything in front of a child and it will not affect him. But, as one psychologist says, "Children are as in deep hypnosis for the first five or six years of their lives, taking in everything for future use."

We all remember, somewhere in our mind, every single thing that has happened to us. Times of trauma at the hands of a mother or father sear deeply. A child beaten, verbally assaulted by a parent or teased unmercifully, will hold this against the parent the rest of his life.

Let us now consider the second of the repressed emotions involved in loss—anger. Why is it so difficult to become aware of anger?

On a conscious level, we fear we will lose the love of our parents if we express anger, or even our very lives should they decide to kill us. We grow up feeling that to survive emotionally we have to hide our anger from the world and ourselves.

On a deeper level, we are still gripped by the childhood fantasy that the wish is the same as the deed. We think if we admit the feeling of hate we will commit murder—hate automatically carries with it the wish to kill. The child and the savage live in the world of magic: even today members of some primitive tribes in Haiti and other parts of the world stick pins through a doll resembling someone they hate, believing the hated one will drop dead, victim of their murderous wish.

But a wish harms no one. We have the right to hate—to wish to kill anyone who hurts us—though not the right to act on that wish. Just as we have the right to desire sexually anyone we find attractive, though not the right to act on that wish if it will hurt others or ourselves.

If we realize thoughts and feelings we believe shameful or dangerous to self-esteem do not have to lead to action, *we free ourselves to feel the rage that is part of every loss, large and small. We do not need to express the rage—it is enough we are able to be aware of it.*

As we can distinguish between a mere wish and an act, we suffer no guilt over a wish no matter how obscene. We are all capable of daydreaming about the most monstrous revenge, the most sordid sexual deed. To deny this is to wear psychic blinders.

After we are aware of anger, we can then decide whether to act on it. We are far more likely to act in destructive fashion if we are *not* aware of anger. We can control conscious feelings but not unconscious ones. The very word "unconscious" means out of conscious control. It is not surprising so many murderers are described by family, friends and neighbors as courteous, charming, soft-spoken individuals who could never kill a fly. They are expert in denying a hidden murderous rage.

When we deny feelings of anger, we are likely to turn the anger either on others who are innocent or on ourselves. We may slowly kill ourselves with a guilt that drives us to drink, drugs, overwork, physical illness or overeating.

Some need the help of a therapist before they can trust themselves enough to become aware of such emotions as jealousy, rage, selfishness, hatred. The goal of psychoanalysis is to bring into consciousness the feelings and fantasies connected to forbidden wishes and the conflicts they create. Intellectual insight alone is not enough. We must *feel* the emotions aroused, emotions believed dangerous to self-esteem. As Yeats wrote, "An intellectual hatred is the worst," a hatred suffered by those unable to become aware of the feelings that underlie the words.

One woman in analysis sometimes casually referred to hatred of a younger sister. "I have hated her since we were children and she stole my dolls," she said.

One day she described in detail a quarrel with her sister over a boy they both liked in high school. She burst into tears and raged, "That little bitch was trying to take him from me!"

Then she said to the analyst in surprise, "I really *felt* my hatred just a moment ago. Deep in my guts. Before, I was just intellectualizing it."

He said, "It usually takes time to allow yourself to feel a deeply repressed emotion that you've been taught since childhood was not admirable to display."

There are moments we feel angry at ourselves—for a *faux pas*, or talking too freely after a few drinks or not dressing in proper fashion for a party. The memory of a *faux pas* may keep us awake as we painfully go over and over it, wondering how we could have been so stupid as to cause such self-humiliation. We are tormented because we feel a loss of dignity.

Such feelings go back to childhood when we wanted the approval of parents but made a mistake and were belittled or ridiculed. As we become aware of our childhood need for approval and attention (every child wants to be Número Uno), as well as the fact our parents probably did make fun us of at times, we accept little failures or errors with good grace, even laugh at ourselves.

That repressed anger may cause harm emotionally and physically, Dr. Karl Menninger has often pointed out. In *Man Against Himself* he noted:

> *Many people are unable to express their hostilities directly or become aware of them. They do not consciously choose self-destruction in preference to a better-directed belligerence. The selection is unconsciously made and they cannot reverse it merely by taking thought.*
>
> *He believes we should "first recognize that the self-destruction is a substitute for hate—for strong aggressive wishes." It is not necessary to turn these aggressive wishes directly, in undiluted form, upon the real object of hate, nor necessary to vent them upon the self, he says, because "there are many other channels—legitimate and even praiseworthy channels—into which to divert the hostilities which cause all of us suffering and many of us death."*

An extreme example of what may happen when rage at a loss is denied was given by Dr. Francis Braceland. A man with such severe arthritis he could not move his right arm went to a clinic where he received a large dose of cortisone. That night the arthritis disappeared and he was able to move his arm freely.

The next morning he got out of bed, went to the kitchen, seized a large knife, returned to the bedroom and slit his wife's throat. He had been denying deep rage at a dominating wife he felt caused him to lose all self-esteem. Instead of facing his rage and leaving her, he unconsciously paralyzed his arm, through arthritis, to keep from murdering her. When the cortisone enabled him to regain use of his arm, he acted on feelings of fury he could no longer control.

Here again we see how an organ of the body can become

involved in a wish—in this man's fantasy he kept wishing to raise his right arm in a killing gesture but repressed the wish. His arm, however, kept reacting to the constant wish to use it to kill, and became physically impaired. When the impairment was removed, the wish erupted.

One man devised a unique way to vent his fury at a loss of self-esteem. He admitted nothing made him feel more unworthy than a snub. When a business partner refused to talk to him over the telephone, he called the police and, giving his name, announced he intended to kill his partner. He had no such intention and the police could do nothing until he acted. This was a way of releasing anger and getting back his self-esteem, as he, too, "took part in the games people play," he explained.

As feelings of repressed anger at a loss are made conscious, the energy freed by lifting their repression is available for the natural aggressive desire to "do" and to "act"—minus hostility. Though there are times, after becoming aware of anger, we may decide to act directly on it.

A husband who felt he had lost self-esteem because of his wife's constant criticism, which he had quietly accepted for years though seething within, asked her one day, "Why do you always blame me for everything that goes wrong? Maybe it *is* my fault sometimes. But I don't claim to be perfect."

Shocked at his unexpected outburst, she was at first silent, then said, "You're absolutely right. I've been a bitch. Forgive me."

One woman married a man who could not have been more charming or romantic all through courtship. But shortly after they married, he started to drink and berate her, at times striking her. Some nights she fled the apartment to sleep in a hotel, fearful of her life. She accepted this physical abuse for a year, not wanting to lose him or her marriage.

Then she went into analysis, using royalties from a successful novel. She discovered she no longer had to accept her husband's cruelty or the loss of self-respect and identity she suffered living with him. One night she gained the courage to say, before he had a chance to get drunk, "I don't want to act behind your back so I'm telling you I intend to leave you and get a divorce."

He begged her to remain, promising he would give up the drinking. But she left, now able to accept the loss of her marriage and of this outwardly charming but cruel man, realizing how destructive it would be to stay—he might one night in drunken violence kill her.

Much daily anger is aroused by the behavior not of those we love but of strangers, especially in crowded cities. We suffer a loss of dignity when someone rudely shoves us in a subway or a thief snatches our wallet. We suffer a loss of valuable time when held up by traffic. Sometimes we act on our anger by fighting back with our fists if physically attacked or with words if someone is sarcastic and arrogant. But most of us find outlets for anger in other ways.

Some use sex as escape, find solace and comfort in the closeness of a warm body, especially if there is the illusion of love. Sex helps for the moment but, like alcohol, drugs or excessive food, it only serves to push anger deeper rather than illuminate its cause and allow it to be felt as part of the mourning process.

Incidentally, tears shed masochistically are a way of denying anger. The woman who bursts into tears at the slightest loss—the breaking of a fingernail, a run in her stocking, the misplacing of a necklace—weeps indiscriminately rather than pinpointing the real targets of her fury. A wholesale anger at the world is denial of childhood anger at a mother and father. To be wildly furious at injustices that exist universally does not solve one's inner conflicts and rarely helps mankind.

It is particularly important to experience anger at a mother and father for the losses and disappointments we feel they inflicted on us in childhood. We should try to become conscious of the full measure of wrath at a parent because of earlier losses. Often the parent was not to blame but our anger, rational or not, lies within, needing to be faced.

One woman, while washing a valuable antique plate her mother had given her, dropped it on the kitchen floor, where it crashed into a hundred fragments. She thought, Why did I do this?

She had been remembering the day her mother had given

her the beautiful plate, but remembering, too, another day when her mother had refused to buy her a blue coat she coveted, because it cost too much, insisting she take a cheap black coat. She had unconsciously broken the antique plate in a moment of pique at her mother for withholding a gift she had wanted far more.

Early feelings of hatred for a parent are difficult to admit because they were so dangerous when they first occurred and they have been so long hidden from awareness. We are brought up as children to believe we must not hate our parents. But we do hate them at times whether we want to or not. The best of mothers cannot help but hurt a child when she tries to discipline him. The most tractable child will feel furious when frustrated in a desire he must control to become civilized.

There are those mothers and fathers who are not lovable. One psychoanalyst observed, "Many people don't like their parents." Some parents are too beset by their own emotional problems to be able to consider the needs of a child. In a sense, they don't deserve the child's love.

Every one of us, at one time or another, has hated our parents as well as loved them. We have to learn not to feel guilty about childhood hatred of parents. Very few of us become Lizzie Bordens. Each time as an adult we hate, then feel guilty, the guilt usually stems not from the present wish alone but the wished-for murders of infancy.

One man became aware he was so filled with childhood guilt he needed the "permission" of some authority figure before he could use his creative talents at times. An author and inventor, he realized this excessive need for permission after a manufacturer persuaded him to develop an invention he had relegated for years to a shelf, not daring to believe it valuable.

"We're all so slugged down by guilt we can't even order a hamburger without feeling we must ask permission," he says. "Alleviating that sense of guilt has to come from within before we can use our talents fully. I think we could all be Einsteins if we could only free ourselves of the need for 'permission' to do or to think."

As we are able without rancor to see our parents as human beings—not monsters or divine souls—we accept their virtues and their faults. To us, they appeared tyrannical at times but we are no longer bound to their orders.

The more we know about our grandparents, the more likely we are to understand our parents. One woman thought of her mother as cringing and submissive, feeling contempt for her, until she realized how dominating her mother's parents were. She pictured her mother as a little girl, then an adolescent, trying to earn the love of two demanding parents, and sympathized with her mother's struggle to survive emotionally.

A man who thought his father overbearing and punitive watched him with his father and saw how similar they were. As his grandfather gave his father an order, this man became aware how such behavior was handed down from generation to generation. He resolved to be more understanding of his two sons.

The adult who cannot face his repressed hatred for a parent, at the time of the parent's death will suffer deeply because of guilt. This is particularly true if death occurs before the healing of rifts; if a parent has not forgiven a son or daughter for marrying someone he considers inappropriate or adopted a life-style he considers outrageous. Or if a child has never accepted a parent who has hurt him.

One woman, thirty years old, had never seen her father after he walked out of the house when she was seven, moving to a distant part of the country. Twenty-three years later, she was staring at his body in a coffin following his death from a heart attack.

She said to a friend, "I didn't shed a tear. Why should I? He didn't love me or he never would have left his family."

Her denial of grief and rage has caused her much unhappiness. She has never been able to love a man—she thinks of a man as an enemy, as she thought of her father. She punishes herself in many ways—drinks too much, overeats, is promiscuous—unaware of her burning rage at the father who dared desert his family, leaving the economic, psychological and social burdens of bringing up two infants on the shoulders of a young wife.

Another woman, thirty-three years old, as a result of therapy was finally able to feel grief and fury at her father, who had left his family when she was twelve to marry his secretary, a younger woman. At first, in her analysis, this woman insisted she adored her father, telling the analyst, "I didn't blame him in the least for leaving my mother. She is a very possessive, dominating woman. He couldn't call his life his own."

One day on the couch, recalling the evening her father had packed and walked out of the house, she burst into tears. Drying her eyes, she said apologetically, "I never cried before at the thought of my father's leaving. I didn't even cry the night he left."

"How old were you?"

"Twelve."

"A little girl of twelve would feel very lost when her father left her," the analyst said.

"My mother didn't cry," she said defiantly. "Why should I?"

"Your mother probably felt like crying but held back her tears," said the analyst. He added, "And your mother wasn't twelve years old, needing a daddy in the house."

"I guess I was angry at him for leaving us," she admitted.

"You were furious at him for daring to desert you—for rejecting you. You have repressed your rage at your father. And you have had a difficult time trusting another man."

She started to accept that her buried feelings of hurt, sorrow and anger had kept her from trusting any man. She never dared allow herself to become emotionally involved with a man, though sexually intimate with several. She spent many psychoanalytic sessions sobbing, releasing a feeling of despair she had repressed for years at feeling rejected, then raging at her father. Finally, she could accept his loss, knowing both he and her mother had done their best to keep the family intact until their own conflicts interfered.

A woman of twenty-seven, whose mother died when she was only three years old, had lived with a deep sense of loss, never knowing why. During her analysis, she discovered not only her hidden grief at her mother's death but her fury at her mother for dying. As a small child, she thought her mother had willfully deserted her, leaving her in the clutches of a selfish stepmother. This fantasy persisted until the analyst helped her become aware of the distortion. She realized she had viewed her mother's death through the eyes of an abandoned, emotionally troubled three-year-old. She was now able to scream on the couch, "How could she do this to me?" and know this was how she had felt when she was three and *was still feeling*.

Dr. Helene Deutsch reports a case in which a young man in his early thirties came for analysis, though he appeared to possess no apparent serious problems. The young man said he could not fall in love, was unable to form friendships, felt no interest in anyone.

During analysis he spoke of the death of his mother when he was five. He recalled he had accepted her loss without any show of feeling. Then he commented that, after she died, he would leave his bedroom door open "in the hope that a large dog would come to him, be very kind to him, and fulfill all his wishes."

He mentioned a dog he once owned who died shortly after the birth of her puppies, leaving them helpless. Deutsch explained that his memories and feelings about his mother had disappeared from consciousness, displaced onto the wish for a new "large dog." Following his mother's death, instead of being able to express a wish for her return and anger at her desertion, his mourning had moved directly, and prematurely, to the phase of detachment. He had not experienced the necessary stages of anger and despair. His yearning for his mother and anger at her death had become locked inside, psychically active though consciously denied. He grew up emotionally impoverished, unable to give love or seek it.

Contrary to the saying "What you don't know will never hurt you," it is what we do not know about our feelings that *will* hurt us. If the phases of mourning are not emotionally experienced, the feelings connected to an early loss do not lose their traumatic power. Despair and anger may remain quiescent but they are ever ready to rise to consciousness, sometimes with ferocity when memories of the loss are stirred, as they inevitably will be, by current losses.

Because of the many years we spend emotionally attached to a mother and father, we will suffer when we lose them. But it is the unacknowledged hatred in the mixed love/hate relationship of childhood that causes us an extra burden of grief.

Ambivalence is the name of the game of life. *And it is the awareness and mastery of the hate in the ambivalence* that enables us to successfully mourn a loss.

Releasing the repressed feelings inherent in the mourning of childhood losses is an important part of a personal psychoanalysis. Dr. Vamik Volkan, professor of psychiatry at the University of Virginia, has developed what he calls "re-grief therapy" to cope with the problem of incomplete mourning. When he finds severe, unresolved grief in a patient, Dr. Volkan takes the bereaved person back in time to experience feelings he has denied so he will be able to accept the loss.

Some authorities in human behavior have suggested working off anger at a loss by hitting a golf or tennis ball or engaging in some other activity. Finding physical outlet for anger is healthier than sinking into a depression. But it is even more rewarding if we can face the hidden reasons for the anger. Then we will more fully enjoy the sport, as well as acquiring new energy from the release of repressed feelings.

It helps to be able to talk about a loss to a sympathetic friend or relative. Sometimes we can hardly stop talking if a loss is deep. Talk is release for anxious feelings. Macbeth says:

> *Give sorrow words; the grief that does not speak*
> *Whispers the o'er-fraught heart and bids it break.*

Writing may be one way of becoming aware of feelings aroused by a loss. Author and journalist Margaret Parton Hussey has faced an unusually high number of losses the past few years, including the death of her eighteen-year-old son, her mother, her husband and several close friends. She has used writing as a catharsis, she says, at times even bursting into tears at the typewriter during parts of her autobiography, the highly acclaimed *Journey Through a Lighted Room.*

"The losses are still there, the ache never heals," she says. "But you accept them as part of the flow of life."

When her son Lemuel (named after her father, the columnist Lemuel F. Parton, who died when she was twenty-seven—the first death to occur in her life) died of leukemia, she says, "I felt as if a giant blow had come up from the earth and hit me in the heart. I told Dr. Donald Tapley, a friend who was Lem's attending physician, 'I'm going to kill myself.' "

She recalls Dr. Tapley, now dean of the College of Physicians and Surgeons, Columbia University, looked at her and said quietly, "Then you will do no credit to Lem."

She survived all her losses, she maintains, because her parents taught her, "Self-pity is the greatest vice; courage, the greatest virtue."

She adds, "If parents don't teach this to a child, by example as well as precept, how can a child blame itself when it goes to pieces after a loss?"

The way a parent accepts a loss influences the way his child will accept losses. If a parent is able to understand his despair and anger at a loss, he will understand these feelings exist in his child when there is a loss. The child automatically copies the way his parents behave in the face of a loss. He benefits not primarily from the words of a parent but from the example set by the parent. Unless a parent can mourn his losses, he will be in some measure responsible for intensifying the normal conflicts of his child.

When a child faces a loss, a parent should encourage him to express grief and anger, sympathize with how he feels. It is psychic cruelty for a parent not to allow a child to mourn a loss. The sadistic fantasies that ensue when a child represses anger may, if intense enough, eventually cause him to destroy himself or others.

A parent should never mock a child's tears or anger at a loss, whether it be the loss of a pet dog, a loss of self-esteem at a poor mark in school or a snub by a playmate.

Some parents try to talk a child out of his feelings of loss. This undermines the natural capacity of a child to tolerate a loss.

Times of illness in childhood will be felt as a loss of health and self-esteem and parents should provide relief from pain and loving care, not show anxious concern out of guilt. Parents should not blame a child for falling ill or blame themselves, as though they somehow should have prevented the illness.

A mother should also understand her child's need to free himself from his attachment to her, his first large loss. To ease this step of separation, mothers usually provide what psychoanalysts call a "transitional object"—a blanket or stuffed animal the child takes everywhere, refusing to part with it. He treats this object as though it were his mother, holding it close for solace, especially at bedtime, for sleep is separation from the world of reality.

There is strong natural desire in every child to be independent even as he wishes to cling to his mother. The wise mother does not encourage him to cling but to explore, as she keeps a watchful eye. She knows the difference between overprotecting a child from her own fantasies of danger and protecting him against real dangers. There is a happy medium between the mother who allows her child to go out into the cold without warm clothing or to stay up late to watch television, depriving him of the rest he needs, and the mother who worries so about her child's every move that he never feels independent, or secure about his sexual or aggressive feelings, but represses them as threats to loss of his mother's love.

There are important times a parent can help a child face what the child believes loss of love. At the birth of a brother or sister, a child is bound to feel rejected no matter how understanding the parents. They can help him regain self-esteem by assuring him of love. If he makes derogatory remarks about the new rival, instead of punishing him they should tell him they know exactly how he feels, that they felt the same way when they watched their mother with a new baby.

During toilet training a mother should give a child the sense his excretory functions are natural rather than shameful. Doctors advise against the use of enemas or suppositories to encourage a child to defecate. Nor should a mother bribe a child to produce, with promises of candy. The proper foods—vegetables, fruits and grains—ensure elimination of waste.

One of the most tragic burdens placed on a child is to be identified with a brother or sister who has died. Vincent van Gogh's parents did this to him. He was named for a brother who died before Vincent's birth. He frequently passed his brother's tombstone, seeing on it the name "Vincent van Gogh." He was born the same day and month exactly one year after his dead brother and was inscribed in the parish register of births under the same number, 29. He eventually committed suicide on the twenty-ninth day of July. The episode in which he cut off an ear and sent it to a woman indicates the depth of the fear of castration that terrorized him.

Children should be gently encouraged to accept frustration, to be creative, to assert themselves not angrily but with realistic aggression. They should be helped to face a certain degree of loneliness.

"The task of mastering the fear of being alone governs the life of most of us," as one psychoanalyst said.

We do not have to feel desperate in our loneliness if we realize excessive feelings of loss, emptiness and helplessness come out of childhood. They are remnants of times we had to separate from our mother. Loneliness reflects the separation blues. "To say good-bye is to die a little," as the old French adage goes.

If we are aware the anguished feelings belong to an earlier era, we can then enjoy *solitude*, which differs from loneliness. No emotional pain is felt in solitude, a conscious choice, whereas loneliness holds the pain of loss and depression. In solitude we do not feel alienated from the self and others but take pleasure in the chance to think creatively. We feel not a loss of identity but an enhancement of the self.

The most important thing to remember when we suffer a current loss, large or small, is not to flee feelings. Fight for the acceptance of the loss by experiencing emotionally all agony. Feel the ache of a loneliness that seems unbearable. Feel the determined wish to get back what we have lost. Experience protest against the affliction visited upon us, express our outraged cries of "Why me?" Feel raging anger at what we think unmitigated injustice, undeserving torture. And then allow the fury to flow through our veins. Recall the times we choked back wrath as we hated with all our being, fantasying the sweet taste of revenge. Remember our guilt at daring to possess what we believed such evil feelings.

Know, too, that the way we react to a current loss, be it a serious one such as the death of a parent or a small one like the insult of an acquaintance, is determined by the way we reacted to the past losses of life, including the small separations.

"It is impossible to accept a loss completely realistically," says Dr. Henriette Klein. "We react to a current loss on the basis of our past losses, past hurts, past disappointments—all our disappointments get equated with losses."

Most of us have had parents unable to mourn their losses fully, so we have to start anew to understand and experience the process of mourning as we follow the advice of the Bible: "Blessed are they that mourn: for they shall be comforted."

In one sense, we have to acquire a new trust in ourselves. Trust is based on self-esteem, confidence in our own judgment. Trust comes out of knowing what we feel. First and foremost, we have to be able to trust our feelings.

Trust grief. Trust hurt. Trust hatred. Trust jealousy. Trust wishes for revenge. Trust greed. Trust all the feelings we have been taught to think of as sinister. For these feelings are as much a part of us as the acceptable "good" feelings.

As we lose fear of the supposedly unacceptable feelings, we better understand ourselves. We use the new understanding to resolve conflicts that have been troubling us, causing us to make an unhappy choice in lover or mate, or to choose a career we do not like.

Those unaware of their deeper feelings may never find a soul they can trust. All the money and success in the world cannot bring trust, as proved by the many who achieve wealth and fame but are lonely and suspicious, without faith in anyone or anything.

Out of trust in ourselves will come the ability to trust others. We are likely to choose a more trustworthy person to love, with whom to live in permanent intimacy. We are apt to trust our decisions as to career or business deal. When we occasionally lose, we will lose gracefully without feeling we wish to die of shame. We will have lost the need to be "perfect."

There will be losses, for they are part of life. There is

always ". . . the heart-ache and the thousand natural shocks that flesh is heir to. . . ."

We have to accept a certain amount of pain along with pleasure. Only the child-mind believes life is one round of joy. As we mourn our losses, our lives become enriched. We no longer live ostrichlike about our true emotions.

Most important, we finally accept the losses of the past that, like monstrous ghosts, have haunted our every current loss, large and small.

And with that acceptance, the sorrow and the fury vanish.

BIBLIOGRAPHY

CHAPTER ONE
The Sense of Loss

Cannon, Walter B. *Bodily Changes in Pain, Hunger, Fear and Rage*. London: D. Appleton-Century Co., 1929.

Lindemann, Erich. "Symptomatology and Management of Acute Grief." *American Journal of Psychiatry*, 101, 1944.

Parkes, C. M. "The First Year of Bereavement." *Psychiatry*, XXXIII (1970).

CHAPTER TWO
How Losses Affect Us

Freud, Sigmund. "Mourning and Melancholia." *Standard Edition*, Vol. XIV. London: The Hogarth Press, 1957.

———. *The Origins of Psychoanalysis: Sigmund Freud's Letters to Wilhelm Fliess, Drafts and Notes, 1887–1902*. New York: Basic Books, 1954.

CHAPTER THREE
The Mourning Process

Abraham, Karl. "Notes on the Psychoanalytical Investigation and Treatment of Manic-depressive Insanity and Allied Conditions." *Selected Papers*. New York: Basic Books, 1953.

Bowlby, John. "Grief and Mourning in Infancy and Early Childhood." *The Psychoanalytic Study of the Child*, Vol. XV, ed. Ruth S. Eissler et al. New York: International Universities Press, 1960.

———. "Processes of Mourning." *International Journal of Psycho-Analysis*, Vol. XLII. (1961).

Deutsch, Helene. "Absence of Grief." *Psychoanalytic Quarterly*. Vol. VI. (1937).

Freud, Anna. "Discussion of Dr. John Bowlby's Paper." *The Psychoanalytic Study of the Child*, Vol. XV.

Spitz, René. *The First Year of Life*. New York: International Universities Press, 1965.

Pollock, George. "Mourning and Adaptation." *International Journal of Psycho-Analysis*, Vol. XLII (1961).

———. "Anniversary Reactions, Trauma and Mourning." *Psychoanalytic Quarterly*, Vol. XXXIX (1970).

———. "Process and Affect: Mourning and Grief." Abridged version of essay presented at the Thirtieth Congress of the International Psycho-Analytical Association, Jerusalem, August 23, 1977.

CHAPTER FOUR
Our First Losses

Horney, Karen. *The Neurotic Personality of Our Time*. New York: W. W. Norton, 1937.

Jacobson, Edith. *Depression*. New York: International Universities Press, 1971.

Kafka, Franz. *Letters to Friends, Family and Editors,* trans. Richard and Clara Winton. New York: Schocken Books, 1977.

Lorand, Sandor. "Adolescent Depression." *International Journal of Psycho-Analysis*, Vol. XLVIII (1967).

Mahler, Margaret. "On Sadness and Grief in Infancy and Childhood." *The Psychoanalytic Study of the Child*, Vol. XVI, ed. Ruth S. Eissler et al. New York: International Universities Press, 1961.

Spotnitz, Hyman, and Phyllis Meadow. *Treatment of the Narcissistic Neuroses*. New York: The Manhattan Center for Advanced Psychoanalytic Studies, 1976.

CHAPTER FIVE
The Rewards of Loss

Engel, G. L. "Towards a Classification of Affects." *Expression of the Emotions in Man*, ed. P. H. Knapp. New York: International Universities Press, 1963.

Friedman, Lawrence J. "Defensive Aspects of Orality." *International Journal of Psycho-Analysis*, Vol. XXXIV (1953).

———. *Psy'cho-a-nal-y-sis: Uses and Abuses*. New York: Paul S. Eriksson, 1968.

Rochlin, Gregory. *Griefs and Discontents: The Forces of Change*. Boston: Little, Brown & Company, 1965.

Stewart, Walter A. *The Secret of Dreams*. New York: The Macmillan Company, 1972.

CHAPTER SIX
Combating Loss Through Creativity

Freud, Sigmund. "The Relation of the Poet to Day-Dreaming." *Collected Papers*, Vol. IV. London. The Hogarth Press, 1921.

Hagglund, T. B. "Dying: A Psychoanalytical Study with Special Reference to Individual Creativity and Defensive Organization." Monograph 6, Psychiatric Clinic of the Helsinki University Central Hospital, 1976.

Klein, Melanie. "A Contribution to the Psychogenesis of Manic-depressive States." *International Journal of Psycho-Analysis*, Vol. XVI (1935).
————. "Mourning and Its Relation to Manic-depressive States." *International Journal of Psycho-Analysis,"* Vol. XXI (1940).
Kohut, Hans. *The Analysis of the Self.* New York: International Universities Press, 1971.
Segal, Hannah. "A Psychoanalytic Approach to Aesthetics." *International Journal of Psycho-Analysis,* Vol. XXXIII (1952).
Winnicott, D. W. "The Depressive Position in Normal Emotional Development." *Collected Papers.* London: Tavistock Publications, 1958.

CHAPTER SEVEN
Overcoming Loss With Laughter

Grotjahn, Martin. *Beyond Laughter.* New York: McGraw-Hill, 1957.
Lewin, Bertram. *The Psychoanalysis of Elation.* New York: W. W. Norton, 1950.

CHAPTER EIGHT
Losses in Growing Up

Freud, Sigmund. "Inhibitions, Symptoms and Anxiety." *Standard Edition.* Vol. XVIII. London: The Hogarth Press, 1957.
Lorand, Rhoda. *Love, Sex and the Teenager.* New York: The Macmillan Company, 1965.
Toolan, James M. "Depression in Adolescents." *Modern Perspectives in Adolescent Psychiatry,* ed. John C. Howells. New York: Brunner/Mazel, 1971.

CHAPTER NINE
Losses of Later Life

Berezin, Martin. "Psychodynamic Considerations of Aging and the Aged: An Overview." *American Journal of Psychiatry,* June 1972.
Szalita, Alberta B. "Psychodynamics of Disorders of the Involutional Age." *American Handbook of Psychiatry,* Vol. III, ed. Silvano Arieti. New York: Basic Books, 1959.

CHAPTER TEN
How to Face Losses

Deutsch, Helene. *The Psychology of Women*. New York: Grune & Stratton, 1944.
Groddeck, Georg. *The Book of the It*. London: Vision Press, 1950.
Menninger, Karl. *Man Against Himself*. New York: Harcourt, Brace & World, 1968.
Ruddick, Bruce. "Colds and Respiratory Introjection." *International Journal of Psycho-Analysis*, Vol. XLIV, 1963.

We all face losses
every day of our lives:

- a friend snubs us or hurts us with unkind words
- the pink slip arrives along with our Friday afternoon paycheck
- after twenty-five years of loyal service to the company, we're forced into early retirement
- we miss a bus or plane
- we lose a wallet, credit card or treasured ring
- the divorce becomes final
- a loved one dies...

Whether they're big or little, life's losses are endless—and no one escapes their inevitable arrival. As world-famous psychoanalyst Dr. Margaret Mahler says: "Growing up is a continuous process of mourning losses." Now, we no longer have to face these losses alone. At last, a book is available that deals thoroughly and directly with the losses that confront us in everyday life.

In *The Sorrow and the Fury*, Lucy Freeman draws on insights gleaned from her own analysis and from talking with psychoanalysts and other experts to fully explore the dynamics of loss. With sympathy and real understanding, she discusses why losses affect us the way they do and how we can handle them.

The Sorrow and the Fury covers everything we need to know about our daily losses and disappointments, including the steps in the mourning process; the difference between natural and unhealthy mourning; and how our present reactions to loss relate to patterns formed early in life. What Lucy Freeman makes dramatically clear for